A DRIFTER IN THE MIND

J. ROBERTS

TATE PUBLISHING & *Enterprises*

"A Drifter in the Mind" by J. Roberts

Published in the United States of America
by Tate Publishing, LLC
127 East Trade Center Terrace
Mustang, OK 73064
(888) 361–9473

ISBN: 1–5988646–5-3

060606

Dedication

This book is dedicated to those whose inspiration and support allowed these words to flow. All of those who've helped have my eternal thanks. The greatest gift you can ever give another is hope. I should know. I spent a number of years without it.

Special thanks go out to Doris, Renee, Deb and Nancy.

TABLE OF CONTENTS

Preface

There are times in your life when you look back with awe and wonder. You can't imagine repeating the things encountered in your past. It eludes you how you survived and thrived through the worst of it. It just shows you how the human spirit is a fragile, yet wonderful testament to mankind's existence. This is about such times, the good as well as the bad.

In America there are many illnesses that inflict her people. Most are termed as medical. They have prescribed treatments and are readily talked about in bars as well as classrooms. There are, however, illnesses which are not discussed. They burden many more households than you would imagine. They are only discussed behind closed doors and doctors' offices. These fall under the category of mental illness and are the most devastating of all. They inflict great internal pain with relatively no external signs. Most people don't even realize that their neighbors are suffering from it.

To those of you who deal with mental illness, I feel your pain. I, unfortunately, have become a veteran of it after many years of dealing with it. This is not a badge that I wear proudly. I only display it out of necessity and shear determination to survive and lead some kind of meaningful life. We do not always choose our struggles. There are times when they are thrust upon us. It is these times that we remain strong for those whom we love. Here is my story.

Gasps of a Suffocated Man

Nov 6

Stored away and locked down tight, a little package sat.
Kept from view but never forgotten, collecting dust and debris
Left for years with use unknown and rarely looked upon.
A greater part of the whole, empty and full together.

Some would think the shell was void. Others know it not.
Some would expect all as well and never give a thing.
Lost and found with purpose lacking, what became the use.
Someday a promise would hopefully commence and lock would fall aside.

Pandora used hers to store all such evil things.
Mine became the keeper of all that I could not have,
or never thought deserved. Watered for years by tears of grief.
Stained by sobbing breaths. Left to wish for a soul who would burn away
the eternal surrounding dew.

Outer member composed of subtle fear, inner one made of cold stone
Combined they made a fortress supreme. Thoughts and feelings secured
from view. Emotion exposed would release pain. Always better to keep
controlled. Some would knock and try to see, effort always fell short.

Years of neglect and mounting abuse, piled against its sides.
Determined to hold up and find a way. Waiting for its time of life.
Periods and years past its place. Dust swirls encircled its corner.
Memories faded and time marched on. Rust protected from the elements.

That is how it sat in place. Disturbed by none who cared.
Hopeless case left aside. Needless baggage for the journey.

With added weight and burden to move, why make the attempt.
Ride out my time and just survive. A break free out of question.

Then the day came at last, the door to the room swung open.
Taken out and viewed at last. Wonderment did await.
Confusion of what it stored and kept. Treasures to be uncovered.
Key in hand with gentleness managed to move the creaking hinge.

Swung wide open with eyes aglow, gasps of breath burst forth.
A wonderment and bright light sprung forth from its sunken depth.
Someone knew the value of the rusty tarnished shell.
Someone knew its glow and warmth determined life inside.

Let out and released it sprang forth and beamed straight into sky.
Freedom finally gave it life, looking to show a path.
Cradled with such soft care, and gently petted touch.
Kind and heartfelt embrace nurtured it back to health.

Reflected back in many fold it now burns intense and pure.
Looking to repay those who kindly brought it out.
Words of thanks and praises for any and all who lent a hand.
Intensity of the love shall never cease. Not to be stored again.

The joys and remembrance of things of old, add to the enhanced motions.
Senses tingled as if youth renewed. Rebirth of mystic sort.
The inner glow worth the cost. Scars and journey not forgotten.
Little ways of thanks shown. Words fall short the gratitude felt.

How do we know our place and ability, if we never have struggled so hard?
A bead of sweat only shows the effort, but the pain determines the cost.
I relive some and absorb the rest. A lesson etched in the soul.
Learn and love as deemed by human form, while always in Creator's hands.

INTRODUCTION

As I have been writing this book I have changed. Every sentence has taught me something about myself. As I go back and read things that I wrote months ago, I find events and situations that still touch and upset me. There has been a great deal of pain associated with my life and this work. This book has been a healing process in its own right; however, that still does not take away from its effect.

It is not an easy thing to write about these kinds of experiences, especially the bad ones. The good times that were funny are easy. The hard times still bother me. Years later the sounds, feelings and smells are still in my mind. I can recall conversations vividly. I know where I was standing and what I said. The same thoughts and fears run through my mind. I can feel the cold and see my breath.

Many people don't understand these things. Those who do have a tear in their eye just as I have one in mine. The brotherhood formed by these things is not one that is celebrated. We do not have picnics and barbecues. We struggle and fight to get through what no one should ever have to face. There is no membership fee, ring or pledge. We have no club meetings. There are only memories and pain that are beyond words.

The support groups and therapy sessions only act as an outlet for us. You speak of these things only in proper forums.

To recall and reflect is a struggle unto itself at times. You do not seek solace in these things. You do not look for others who go through these things. They have the same problems and troubles as you have. You deal as best you can and hope that the next day is better. You never say that things could be worse. That is because you know that they could. You have seen it.

The good news here is, with advances in medicine and treatment schemes, things have gotten better. Over the centuries, mental illness has never really been treated properly. Only in modern times have we advanced enough to be able to look at it in a better and more realistic light.

I have seen many changes in the time frame that I have had to deal with these things. I am happy to report that things are getting better. However, the overall problems associated with this are still the same. In time, I hope that future generations do not have to go through the things that I have had to. With any luck, medicine and treatments will be greatly advanced.

In writing the stories and events, I have found that I was not only was a witness to these things; I was a willful participant. It took me many years and numerous therapy sessions to realize this. In the midst of such things you become an active member.

I started this book as a way to write about things that I had seen with my ex-wife, Terry. I will finish this book as a collection of learning experiences about myself. I have roamed forgotten places in my past and present. I have considered many things about my future. The therapy within this book has allowed me to look again for what makes me tick, what makes me special. Most importantly, though, what makes others unique and different.

In the search that I have been on, I have found many dark places in myself that I never knew existed. Once found,

I explored them. At that point I learned that I did not even know myself, let alone anyone else. It is enlightening to find that after many years, you have just discovered many things about yourself; how you felt, what you thought, why you feel the way that you do about things.

That is all part of the healing process each one of us has to go through. On any given day, when you think you know how you feel, step back. Wait a minute and check again. You may find that you really have no clue what your real feelings are. Stop and look. It may do you some good.

As I write and add to this book I look inside myself and try to find the essence of my thoughts and feelings. I try to convey the truth in the clearest possible light. At times the truth appears clouded. Upon closer inspection, though, it clearly comes into view. You just have to look harder.

Many areas in our lives are gray. Black and white is usually well defined. Most people live their lives somewhere in the middle. No matter where you fit in on the gray scale, there is always a greater truth. You may not agree with its interpretation, but it is there. If you look deep inside yourself you will find it. Forget the rest and just concentrate on what is real. The truth is just an eye blink away. Close your eyes and open your mind and heart. It will appear right before you. In an instant, all of the confusion disappears and reality sets in, magically.

When you finish reading this book put it down and go hug your kids. Let them know how special they are. Hug your spouse or significant other. Be grateful that you have the ability to do that. There are many others who don't. Try not to take for granted that privilege. If nothing else, remember that others suffer quietly all around you. They may seem normal and okay, but that does not necessarily equal the truth. Think about it.

I say this because I have been there. I know what it is

like to not be able to see someone I loved. The essence of the person was gone. Sometimes for a short period, other times for much longer lengths of time. To deal with these things is a lesson in life itself. Take nothing for granted. When you think things will last, they may not. Life itself is a fleeting moment. Savor it.

As you read this book keep in mind one more thing. Remember that all of the stories and events are true. They actually happened. This is not a fictional work that was manufactured in someone's head. These are real events that happened to real people.

These are events that encompassed a real family trying to live their lives. As you read, look around at your own family. Imagine going through these things with them. Consider what it would do to you. Consider what it would do to them. Think about the number of American households that actually experience these things.

Mental illness is not a subject that is readily or normally talked about. You may be surprised at the number of families that deal with these kinds of things. Your neighbor may be one. For all that you know other family members may have been dealing with these issues for years and you never knew. I can tell you that they are not going to tell anyone unless they feel they have to. It is not a topic for discussion around the table at Thanksgiving, Christmas or any other holiday.

I leave you to experience this book. Remember that for you, these are only stories. They are only words on paper. To me, they are a reality that will live forever in my thoughts and mind. That is why these things carry so much weight with me. Over the years they have become an integral part of me; whether I wanted them to or not.

There are a lot of tears on these pages. It is my hope and desire that these words may, someday, somehow, save someone. I have always felt that I have endured these things for years for a greater purpose. Maybe the writing of these things and the telling of the stories is it. I can only hope that this belief is true.

"A cry is a breath of your soul's inner shine."

SURVIVING

"We are quiet and crawling to get to our place,
but our tears are just as genuine
No shouting or screaming shall ever occur, only
grateful silence and peace of mind."

BEGINNING OF DAY LIGHT

After many years and many episodes I went to bed one night. Things were the same as they always had been. I closed my eyes and drifted off to sleep. Somehow in my dreams a fundamental change occurred in me. I am not sure exactly what happened. All that I can tell you is that I woke up a different person. It possibly stemmed from the final connection of my mind, body and soul.

Simplicity

Feb 23

On a canvas of blue and black, the pastels spread across.
They reach from ground to touch the heavens, changing ever constantly.
The crimson ball will slowly rise, to greet awakening souls.
The sleep is wiped from straining eyes. Vision a chore of morn.

With height the orange fades to yellow and force will be felt.
Then warming feeling envelopes all who encounter happiness at the entry.
When teary-eyed lives are on the edge, the rebirth may give them hope.
When rain departs and clouds break down,
gentle blue softens the struggle.

Impressions show a chance and change that maybe things are improving.
The simplest thing that is always free. Cost a great value to behold.
For every morning, the show repeats itself. Act one, scene one, new day.
In this life many things cost a great deal. Not in money but in pain.

But we are given precious gifts, which we forget are always free.
Consider these treasured times, then bad only seems fleeting.
A warm summer rain, a star-filled night, a full moon over water.
A sunrise and sunset, a waterfall, a child's laugh, an old man's tale.

The richest man may buy the object, but never pay for these.
God makes sure that what we need is always there for the taking.
A kiss or hug is a given thing, a compliment for the mind.
Do not judge the life's value in coins but in derived worth.

In the end we carry nothing when we cross the spiritual plane.
We empty pockets, strip our worth to what is soulfully carried.
At the gate they check the sum of all the objects stored.
It is tallied by a meter of life and not marked in a digit in gold.

When in doubt, follow the heart, the soul is close behind.
To stray away from what is real, places you in the lost voids.

Await a search of truer things when unsure and confused.
Just remember keep it simple. Isn't that always the best?

New Dawn

In the morning when I woke up the grass was somehow greener. The sun shone just a little bit brighter than before. The sky seemed a bit bluer as well. These things and many others seemed to change over night. Why you ask? I have no clue.

As I went down stairs and made coffee, the house had a different feel. I realized for the first time in my life that I did not belong there. I had lived there many years. It was my house. It just wasn't a home anymore. It was just a bunch of walls with a roof over it.

When I first saw Terry that day, I realized that she was different as well. I found that I didn't want to kiss her. I didn't want her to touch me. I didn't want anything that had been routine the day before. I couldn't figure out what had changed. Something had, drastically.

I felt a little hungry. I went to the cabinet and grabbed a box of cereal. It was a box of Life cereal. I looked at the box. I started to cry. I thought, "Why are you crying? Is it because the box says Life?" I couldn't figure it out. After I poured the cereal in a bowl and poured in milk, I ate it and drank my coffee. This was the same routine that I had been doing for years. I shaved and then climbed in the shower.

While soaping up I started to cry again. Why? This time I couldn't stop. All of the frustration through the years had built up inside of me. The resentment, anger and pain had taken a hold of me. I was not one to cry in the past. I was sobbing now.

After a little bit I composed myself and started to get

dressed for work. I gathered my things for the day and started the car. I drove about one mile and started to cry again.

This was nuts, I thought. Was I losing my mind?

The grieving process that has started in me has built up over the years. At this point it is long overdue. After extended periods of emotions, though, I feel better. To release and finally accept this has at the same time drained me and freed me. Every day since then I feel a little bit stronger. I accept things a little bit easier. I am healing.

Every day I would struggle through tears as many varied things would spark my reactions. Not being very good with emotions, I didn't understand. I had never been one to cry in the past but I was very emotional at this point.

Early mornings seemed to bring out the worst in me. I dreaded the rides to work and gauged my healing progress by how far I could get before I began to tear up. The day I actually got into work before it occurred was a proud one, in a warped sort of way. It was progress for me at least.

Little steps meant I was finding out who I was. I knew I was a genuine, gentle sort of person. It was just never allowed to come out. Being on the defensive constantly never allowed who and what I was to flourish. That is very disheartening, I must tell you.

So on it went with the tears and emotional swings for weeks. I didn't understand what was happening to me. I had never acted like this before. I had always been a levelheaded person with a constant exterior. I had always held my emotions in check before. Now, though, they were unraveling.

After a while of this I decided to talk to someone. The question was who? I had never sat down and discussed this with anyone outside of doctors. To come out and talk brought about every fear that I had in me. I thought about it for a while and decided on someone. I tell you now how it was probably the hardest and best thing that I have ever done in my life.

Let the Cat Out Of the Bag

I went to work and decided to call the person. I had somehow gotten through the day. It was later in the afternoon and she called and said she would be over. We had known each other for a few years, but I had never told her about any of these events. I had always kept this to myself.

We found a quiet little spot out of the way and we began to talk. I told her that I didn't know how to start, so the beginning was as good a place as any. I began to tell her my story. I began to cry again but knew that I had to finish. I enlightened her as to these things and she was taken aback. When I finished I realized that I should have done it years ago. I felt a little better. Now, though, someone else knew.

Although I had let a great weight be lifted off of my shoulders I felt guilty. I had told someone else the truth. I spoke of things that I had never told another living soul. This was a first for me. To actually open up and talk was a new concept for me. After many years it is not easy. I find that I only really talk when I have had to. There was no one there to listen. Through the years I had never bothered looking for someone. Who would listen to this anyway?

Dealing with It

The strangest part is the fact that when going through all of this, you never really understand what is happening. You are so caught up in the events; you never see the big picture. At the end, you are just happy to have survived and come out of it in one piece. Once it is all done and you have time to reflect, you find that it hits you.

In my case, it took years to come about. It had built up over time. At that point I had been deeply scarred. I am still finding the marks now. I never knew that I had them. You get so used to these things that you just accept it.

The word dealing is actually a lie. You never deal with

it. You avoid, deny and fool yourself. Then down the road, you pay. That is the reality. Over the last few years I have woken up many mornings and actually dealt with it. I get depressed, I cry and I cope. I resent and find the strength within to handle it. Now I am dealing with it.

"When you have sat in an empty room your whole life,
you never learn to look for the light switches. They
would illuminate the emptiness even more."

Reality Sets In

As you come out of these things you begin to realize what has happened. A clearer vision of events and damage takes hold. It has been a long time since I have seen the truth. The reality of the events and the current situation begins. It is a sign of things changing and me getting better.

The denial of the facts starts to disappear. I see things in her and in me that I never saw before. I know when the bipolar rears its ugly head and I know that things are not right. These things never happened before. I sense when I should just start to back away and times when I should run like hell. I always stood there in the past with a stupid look on my face.

I don't think it was a form of shock that prevented me from seeing things. I think it was more of a self-denial as to the realities. A kind of self-preservation attempt if you will. Hide in a shell and maybe the problem will go away stance. If that makes sense? The problem was, it never did.

What is sad is that she doesn't know that I see these things now. She still takes the stance that she always did. Now I don't argue. I realize how futile it is. You can't win an argument if you don't know the truth. No matter how loud you shout, you're still wasting your time. I don't argue back. I walk away.

There is a down side to all of this. It is the fact that you see the truth. You see how other couples are truly interacting. The love, sharing and caring that were never a part of your relationship. It brings tears to my eyes constantly. To walk through a mall or a store and see other couples to this day hurts me. It took me a long time to go into a public place without tearing up at least once.

Not that there wasn't any interacting between us. It was just diminished and not in the true sense of the words. Our interactions involved a more mutated reality that with any luck is gone from my life. The sharing was limited and selected. It was based upon boundaries that were established through years of false realities that we had both accepted.

As I get a better look at us I see how things really are. I see how with a simple twist of the facts the mutation occurs. It is slight at first, but grows rather quickly. It is like a germinated seed that grows into a mighty tree. Once it starts down its path, it just keeps growing.

Push Me Pull Me

In every marriage and relationship there must be a give and take. It should be roughly equal. It never is. You just get it as close as you can. In these things, the caretaker has to give to allow the other individual to take. You find yourself constantly accepting and sacrificing to allow the relationship to continue. Even though you think you are in control, you are not. The other person and their actions dictate all of your actions and responses.

Once I started to heal, I decided that this process would end. I felt that therapy for Terry and I was a necessity to the survival of any relationship that we might have had. We needed marriage counseling as well as therapy for each one of us individually.

Since this was met with a barrage of no's and an insistence on the fact that I was trying to destroy her, I felt that the point was moot. I had been in therapy for a few months. I knew that no matter how much better I could make myself, I was only one piece of the puzzle. As in any relationship, both parties must agree to resolve problems. If only one works toward the resolution, it will never be reached.

With a stern no, and her back arched up, she hissed at me. I saw the claws come out and knew that I had a fight on my hands. I also knew that if we were to make it, I had to fight. I had to convince her that therapy, counseling, and communication were the only way.

We had been communicating a lot since this all started in me. I noticed that. Unfortunately, the increase in words did not equate to an increase in healing. We still fought about the same things daily. We each took the same stances that we had the day before. There was no progress.

I began to wonder if it was me. Then one day, Terry started to argue with my oldest son. Their argument sounded so familiar. I had had that same fight with her the day before. I had heard every response that the oldest made. I had heard every response Terry made. They argued the same way and he made the same points as me. I sat back and pulled up a chair and watched the show. It was very entertaining. I closed my eyes for a while and listened.

After a while, I saw the frustration in his face. I knew how he felt. The same logic and arguments had led him nowhere. He stood there the same that I had many times before. It is funny how at that point I realized that maybe it wasn't me. To take it a step further I asked a third party about it. They responded the exact same way as I had. It was then I knew.

Up, Up, And Away

At this point I realized that this argument was futile. I had for years beaten my head against a wall. I was annoyed, tired, frustrated and just fed up. I only had three choices left. The first being to just ignore what I now knew was wrong and continue to live my life as I had been in the past. The second was try to get her to see the light and keep fighting to get her into therapy. Lastly, throw in the towel and start making plans to get on with my life.

This is where it gets hard. I had had enough of living this kind of lifestyle. I couldn't handle things any more if they wouldn't change. I knew this. Some change was in the cards. How much was to be determined.

To ignore things was out of the question. I wanted change for the better. That was a given. I was going to get that much, one way or another. My only two choices left were stay and try to get her to change, or leave.

Staying was getting harder by the day. I had fought long and hard. I wasn't sure of what she wanted from me. I knew that I wanted resolution. Everyday for months we argued about the same things. We each took the same stance that we had the day before. We argued the same way and it never got us anywhere.

I asked her constantly to go with me to therapy, a marriage counselor, or anything else that I could think of that might help us. She always told me that it had never worked in the past and it wouldn't work now. It had never worked in the past because she had her problems and I was codependent. Now though things had changed. She still had her problems, but I was fighting codependency. I was determined to move forward, with or with out her!

CROSSROADS

As you travel through life you find that you have many choices. Some are very easy and enjoyable. Others are the most painful things that you must ponder. Knowing that the final outcome will be devastating and hurtful only makes it that much harder. I was standing at a crossroad.

The fork to the left had a minor air of hope. It was the fork that showed me hanging on. We still cared a lot about each other. It was a matter of at what cost I would continue this. When you love someone you must decide at what cost to continue the relationship.

I had put things on hold over the years just to try to make things work. I was beginning to get tired of this. I knew that eventually I had to put myself first. This was beginning to get more evident as time went on. Little things that I had struggled to gain were not worth the effort anymore. When she dug her heels in and fought me over simplistic choices, I started getting fed up.

We had come so far, yet I knew that we could have gotten even further. I had never minded sacrificing in the past. I began to wonder what I was giving up, though. The harder the battles became to fight, the less I wanted to fight them. You reach a point where the effort doesn't equal the gain.

This is when a decision has to be made. The best thing that I have always done in the past is list out the good and bad points on a topic. I honestly try to come up with every good thing about a subject that I can think of. Then I turn around and work on every bad thing.

After I do that, I go back and read my lists. I try again to come up with anything else that comes to mind. Usually one argument jumps out at me and I find that in my heart, that is the way to go. Only a few times was the choice split right down the middle. They are the hardest, but they are few and far between.

After my final decision, I inevitably know what I have to do. I just start the process of doing it. Once things are in process, they become easier to keep going. It is just like pushing a car; once you get it moving, it rolls much more easily. The hardest part is getting it rolling.

Caretakers

It may be hard to understand this, but the longer that you deal with these things, the more likely you are to continue. In time you develop a syndrome that allows you to adapt and adjust to these things. Before you know it, this seems normal. It usually takes an outsider to alert you to the problems. I myself had no idea anything was inherently wrong. A "normal" life gets built around all of the fallacies and mutated truths created in this existence.

Certain characteristics and traits allow for the continuation of these things as well. It is fair to say that certain people adapt and thrive to these things. After a while, it becomes second nature. Once you are involved and accept this, you almost become part of the problem. I have found myself contributing to her problems by not stopping things. You allow and aid in certain activities that should never get started. It is only now after I have started to heal that I can see things that I never knew or thought of.

The word "no" was never in my vocabulary. I was just as guilty as her. I never realized it. You become complacent. You learn to fault yourself and constantly make do with the things that you have. You never want or expect better. In order to force someone into treatment, you must make a stand. If you are not capable, it never happens. Consequently you never get it.

This dysfunctional nature takes over all aspects of your life. You are constantly compromising and adjusting things to benefit the other person. In order to maintain tranquility in the house, you will do things that you know you shouldn't do. This doesn't solve the problem. It just keeps the peace. Or so you think.

Characteristics of Caretakers

It takes a unique breed to deal with these kinds of things. Certain social and maybe psychological events or traits have to be evident. Most people when dealing with these things run away from fear. How can you handle behavioral issues such as these?

Actions and reactions constantly occur that are way out of the ordinary. Words, anger, motions physical behavior and ramblings happen constantly. Huge amounts of energy are wasted just keeping the person out of trouble. Sometimes you can't. Sleep is lost and many chances are taken. It involves a greater understanding of impossible scenarios which are an everyday occurrence. There are certain people, though, that naturally are drawn and receptive to these kinds of things.

These abilities may be caused by events and/or traits. They may come about through upbringing, personal experiences and environment. In any event, they must be at least partly present for this dysfunctional existence to occur. Once they are present, they are very difficult to remove and overcome. It takes many years to eradicate them. In some cases it is impossible. Only a certain degree of control is sometimes achievable.

Traits of Caretakers

An independent or self-reliant nature is a primary ingredient. If this is not readily apparent, it will be. You will constantly deal with things yourself. You must always look out for the other person and take control of numerous situations to keep them out of trouble. You may not be the best person to determine the proper course or action. You are not willing to ask or seek help, though. This will eventually be your undoing.

An independent person is more likely to be introverted. They will look into themselves to handle things and be less likely to talk to others about crucial matters. Internal strength is usually drawn upon. External resources are not normally used. Although self-reliance may be an asset that is much sought after, it may be more trouble than it is worth. When you never naturally look for help, you never get it.

In the midst of these things you can very easily become isolated. This only continues the problems. Not to be able to turn to others eventually causes you not to bother looking for help. You get used to going it alone. Eventually, you prefer it.

Inferiority is a dangerous trait to have as well. It causes you to believe that you don't deserve better. You don't seek help. You expect the worst. You do not seek to improve things. You believe others should have better. Not yourself, though. You accept your fate and believe that you have caused these things. This plays into all of the other problems. That is why these things are perpetuated. They do not cease until an outside source intervenes.

Alcoholism and drug abuse in the family only prepare you for a road to self-destruction. When you live with others who have substance abuse issues, you become codependent. You aid and continue this process. When you are brought up as a child and grow into this, you never learn the difference and better behavior. You are accustomed to this. You never seek help or a better life. These things have been instilled in you.

Mental illness in the family also prepares you for

self-destruction. To see these things every day gives you the impression of normalcy with them. It is a very difficult reality to break. If you don't have an external influence, it may not occur.

Here is an example of the mindset that gets imbedded into you. I wrote this before my real healing process began. It illustrates the frame of mind that most going through this have. That is why things are perpetuated.

NOTE TO A FRIEND

The great mystery of life is the meaning to our existence. We all seek the answers. Only a chosen few find them. Each of us has our place and it is up to us to find it. Once found then what? I know where I belong. It is among those who do not belong. I have seen many things, dark and distant, but true. That is home to me.

I find it funny how many fear the night and the silent unknown. I thrive in it. I listen to the sounds that you do not hear. The quiet motions of many things. Most of which you have no knowledge. When I walk, I make no sound. Many have said how I sneak up on them. It is habit to move like the wind, intentionally and without prejudice. To blend in and not be known. To be silent and deliberate is my way. Strong, yet as wispy as a shadow. There but actually not.

The pagan belief has deemed me a falcon. Silent and deliberate. A lone traveler who keeps a clear eye and a sharp mind. Away from the norm. In the canopy, out of sight yet, most assuredly there.

There are many things in this world meant for all. There are some, though, meant for a few. To travel through life is a journey all of us must take. Some of us are meant to travel in the pack. Among many others in safety and security. Others are meant to travel alone.

If you are a soul meant for a pack, you belong with others.

You thrive and soar with the groups that you reside in. I am not. I am meant to walk alone.

Softly and silently through the night I go. In the shadows, away from the light that you huddle around. I do not understand your ways, as you do not understand mine. It is not that I don't long to be with you and yours. It is that I do not belong there. That is why I thrive and soar in my world. As you soar in yours.

Understand me when I say this. Some of us are meant for the black. Others are meant for the light. I never meant any harm. I will return to the dark recesses. I came out to see the world as you see it. It does not suit me. Each of us has a destiny. Each has a place that we were designed by God to take, rightfully. You were designed to love and live. To bring joy to others and share life. To be beacon of light for others to find.

I was made to reside in the dark corners, into worlds that you can barely imagine. It is my home and where I belong. I do not have a place in your world. In my world, I am strong and secure. In your world I am weak and unsure. I always have been a creature of the night. I always will be. I travel and see things meant for only those molded for such an existence. Maybe that is why I write of these things. So the rest of you can understand.

You do not belong there. I will not take you there. Only through my words can you see it. Like a window into another existence. You look through the glass, but are never affected by the elements. You touch the pane and feel the cold. You have nothing to fear on your side.

As I fade into the mist, remember that our paths crossed and for an instant, we were friends. Now, though, we are just travelers on different roads. Searching for answers. Seeking shelter from the rain and wind. As my words drift away, I have only one wish. May you find what you are looking for. Into the darkness and shadows must I go, again.

Salvation

A caretaker can only be saved by one of a couple of ways. Usually it happens when someone external breaks the continuous cycles that they are in. It could be through acts of kindness, befriending them, or just getting them away from these things for a while and seeing another way. This is usually how it occurs.

Another way that the caretaker syndrome can be broken is by the person himself just becoming fed up with this existence. This is not normally the case. Most caretakers don't know any better. They accept their fate. To become fed up means to want to experience better.

The last way is through illness or disease or death of the individual being taken care of or the caretaker himself. A hospital stay or a long separation may jolt the caretaker into a state of reality. This is the least common way. It does happen, though.

Outer Space

Once the caretaker realizes that things on the outside are better, he is receptive to that existence. There is a great tendency to revert back to the bad habits and continue the codependent syndrome. With a lot of time, patience, and effort they may be overcome.

It is the equivalent of seeing a light bulb come on. The vision of better and the ability to reach it are ever enticing. The thoughts of good days and a normal life are like a breath of fresh air. You feel like you just stuck your head above water, and can for the first time take a deep breath.

This sense is like a rebirth. At first it seems almost unbelievable. After a while, though, you can see that it is real. I have found in myself that it took me back. I had to rub and blink my eyes. It was amazing.

There is a down side. It is the realization of all of the

wasted time in this existence. You think why did I do that to myself for so long? Why did I endure this? Why didn't I see this earlier?

You have to learn not to torture yourself, though. It is not an easy thing to overcome. The journey itself would devour many. Just to struggle and survive is a testament to those who go through this. That is what you have to learn to keep in mind. Remember the good and forget the bad.

Every day I have to work on not beating myself up for going through this. I have to concentrate on the fact that I overcame. That is what caretakers must do. It is best not to harp on the time spent in the past. It is the ability to look forward to the things that are to be enjoyed in the future. That is part of the healing.

The other thing that I find myself doing is looking behind me. This may sound trivial but consider that for some of us the journey has been long and will continue well into the future. The act of looking behind you and seeing how far you have come lends strength to the journey that is left ahead of you. It is the ability to gather strength and continue when weary. I do this all of the time. Others just don't understand what it takes sometimes to continue.

Those who have never had to struggle this hard for so long have no idea how worn out you can actually get. There are times when quitting doesn't seem like such a bad idea. That is until you think and look and see what has been overcome. You think about going back to what you were. That is the exact reason it is vital to keep going forward. I never want to go back.

Light at the End of the Tunnel

As you progress and heal, you find that there is light at the end of the tunnel. The snowball effect of wanting more and better continues until healing is relatively complete. Every day that I heal and don't lose ground is a good day. I occasionally loose my footing, but I fight and claw my way back. I accept the fact there are days when this will happen. I expect that. I also know that I will get back any lost ground.

It is the end of the journey that I seek. The struggle that I must overcome only adds credence and value to the effort. It is self-gratifying when I see who I was and what I have become. I am not there yet, but I know that I am well on my way to getting there.

Struggles to overcome make the person. Character is defined that way. I look at others who have that struggle. I respect and help them when I can. They help me. It is a process that aids all concerned.

Angels

10 Feb

An angel does so many things it is not always known.
They surely help the little ones until they are full grown.
In sickness they are there to comfort illness in its ways.
They give their breath to those of us who live suffocated days.

You think that they would hide away because of unknown strife.
An angel would stand proud to say I carry you through life.
In books they write and preach of things and talk of beings winged.
An angel uses so much more. Its voice of hope does sing.

Just listen close to the wind and hear the chorus loud.
For recital commences everyday and makes the father proud.
A clap of thunder tells the world an angel wears a pin.
Forgiven acts of long ago release their trial of sin.

Cross To Carry

Each of us has his cross to bear. The cross may be alcoholism. It may be drug abuse. It may be any number of problems or conflicts. Always remember, though, to carry it with dignity. Carry it with tears in your eyes. Carry it with the hope of the future. For whatever your reason, just carry it. These may sound like simple words. However, they come with a lot of pain attached. If you can't carry your cross, then drag it. In either case, move forward. All attempts to reach out to another soul should be thusly attempted. Not just to possibly save them, but maybe yourself.

The strength that you find in yourself to overcome also aids in many other things in your life. You find that the ability to remain strong and persevere allows you to handle things that you never thought were possible. Personal and business interactions become that much greater. Others see your ability to handle situations that they never could. I have found this at work.

The struggles that you face are 24 hours a day seven days a week. That is what makes them so difficult. You cannot leave them at any door. They stay with you all of the time. Even when you are sitting on a beach looking at the water, your thoughts and memories still haunt you. That is what makes this as difficult as it gets.

If you ever choose to run, it is worthless. You can't run away from these things, and you can never hide. That is why they must be dealt with; if not today, then tomorrow. They will never go away until handled properly. That is all part of the cross.

I have found that my cross is myself. That is the reality that all codependents must come to. We must realize that more often then not we are our own worst enemies. I constantly have to work on my beliefs about myself. I have realized that I do have self-worth and that I am a good person.

Many people deny that they carry a cross. That is their undoing. To deny is only to add weight to it. Denial begins a process that will eventually drop them to their knees. To deny the reality of the cross is the act of lying to others as well as yourself.

I may struggle with my cross, but it is my cross. The characteristics of it are unique. I carved out the knotholes and placed the splinters there. Over the years I have nicked and scarred it. I made every inch of it. I let others dictate to me how much I should add to it and when.

Now I am chipping away at it. Over the last six months it has become lighter. It is still heavy, but I am getting stronger. I do my best. I have made it a point every day not to add to it. I may have a bad day where I do not lighten it, but I make sure not to add. That is the healing process at work.

The Value of Tears

Nov 24

Some men don't know the value of tears.
The shedding of pain. The releasing of fear.

A simple thing occurs as the water falls down.
It comes from the soul and drops to the ground.

Usually it is slowly. But sometimes is fast.
Hard to reduce brought about by the past.

Many do it in private away from the crowds.
Some do it in public. Worn as a shroud.

I prefer with a loved one. With comfort and care.
Surely out of view and away from a stare.

It is an interesting process. A rebirth of the soul.
Release of emotion with cleansing the goal.

A good morning cry is always the best.
Starts off the day after a night time of rest.

A human endeavor. But animals join in.
A sad little concert for the effort of sin.

God created crying for many reasons I know.
An act of rejoicing. A method to grow.

People always look at the matter with shame.
No one at fault but all are to blame.

As natural as breathing. Simple in design.
Wholesome and truthful. Driven by time.

Uses unlimited. With causes as such.
A death, loss or gain, is a matter of touch.

Think more of the effort. A reality we share.
Look up not down. An act out of care.

I leave you this thought. Step light through your time.
A cry is a breath of your soul's inner shine.

Everyday Trials

The hardest aspect of all of these events is the everyday trials. Some days are quiet. Other days grate at your every nerve. You never know what kind of day you will have when you wake up in the morning. It is funny how you can see a good day go terribly wrong within a matter of minutes.

Special Days

Special days of the year are the ones that suffer the most. When you hope that a birthday or anniversary will be a good day, it can turn out bad. I find myself not asking for perfection. I just want peace. This may sound simple. There are times, though, when you are asking the world for such a simple request. These times tear at you heart strings.

My birthday falls in the scope of the episode time frame. It has fallen victim to these things too many times in the past. I almost at this point dread the day. That is a sad thing. I have never asked for much myself. All that I want is just a quiet day. No card, cake or present, just peace. That to me doesn't seem like an outrageous request. I guess maybe sometimes it is.

Our wedding anniversary also suffered through the years. Last-minute changes in things have always affected it. This is one of the many things that you have to adjust to and accept when dealing with these things.

Luckily, everyone else in the household doesn't suffer the same fate. Their birthdays either fall before or after the episode time frame. That allows the rest to be celebrated in a normal atmosphere. At least that is a blessing!

Rolling With the Punches

Many days you just have to deal with the mood swings and the changes in attitudes. Hour to hour you could be facing entirely different situations. In the course of a day I have seen multiple swings in every direction. You go to bed at night almost exhausted sometimes.

I laugh at others talking about mood swings or other such things. I tell them to deal with it for ten weeks straight and then come back and talk to me. They scratch their heads and walk away.

When I am told that someone I know is moody, I have to look really hard to see what they're talking about. At times I can't even see it. I have experienced tidal waves. A little rough surf doesn't bother me. I just ask what mood swing?

In the midst of problems you learn not to add to the troubles. You try to subdue problems and just keep things calm. This is usually harder than it sounds. Just a calm, clear tone and voice works sometimes. Other times, you are out of luck no matter what.

Through all events, you must keep a clear and level head. These things will grate at your nerves. Some days it is much worse than others. At the end of the day, others get to go home and relax and settle down. Those of us who deal with these things daily are home. There is no escape.

I have found myself going out for walks just to get away for a while. A quick hike or short walk clears the head and prepares you for your next adventure that is only around the corner. These little tricks help you keep your sanity when all others around you lose theirs.

Making Sense Out of This

The one thing that I have learned is that there is no reason to try to make sense out of all of this. It is much easier to just go with the flow and not justify these things. Most episodes and incidents have no rhyme or reason. There is no logic or master plan.

This wreaks havoc on trying to plan for future events. The best that you can hope for is to be somewhat ready for whatever awaits you around the corner. Preplanning is a good idea. Flexibility is a necessary asset. Luck is a valuable commodity. Any combination of the three is even better.

Over the years a sense of humor has become essential. I do not think that I could have gotten through things if I had not had that. To be able to laugh heals your own heart and soul. It keeps you medically in better shape. It also takes away the tension that inevitably builds up when dealing with these situations.

The other thing that I learned is that it makes no sense to discuss these things with people who have no training or experience in these matters. Often I find that laymen just don't understand the scope of things. They will try to offer advice and assist. That usually does more harm then good, though. We learn very quickly whom to trust and whom to go to for aid.

Day by Day

It may sound simple but the easiest way to handle things is just to go day by day. If you just take one 24-hour time period and handle that, then you find the days go by and you have handled many more things than you would have thought you were capable of.

It is never a good idea to judge yourself for the actions and events on any given day. Sometimes the stress and your nervousness cause problems. That is to be expected. We all have bad days.

Frequent breaks are a necessity. If you can get away and have a day to enjoy things that you love doing, you should. It is a much-needed respite. These times allow you to come back and handle things with a clear mind and capable heart.

Since every day is different, take one at a time. Some days are good. Some days are bad. You never know what you will have in front of you until it occurs. If nothing else it keeps it interesting.

At the close of a day, never assume that tomorrow will be the same. I have seen drastic changes and swings in a very short period of time. The cycles that occur give you some idea of what to expect. This is not always the case. At times a flat line in any direction can occur.

Eventually things end, though. Sooner or later the whole episode process comes to a close. It either runs its course or hospitalization happens. In any event, things calm down and a relatively normal existence begins again. With luck, it will last long enough to recuperate from the last traumatic events.

Here is a note that I wrote to my attorney. This is but one example of what I am trying to say. These events occurred far too frequently for me. However, until the entire process unfolds, you have to learn to deal with things and find a way to survive.

To whom it may concern,

I guess I am writing this to express how I feel. You may take these words any way you wish.

Throughout a long stretch of time I decided my course and have accepted things will happen and events will occur. That is what makes a struggle and defines character. Easy does not create soul. Difficult shapes the spirit. It is not only the fact that you survive an ordeal. It is the manner in which you walk through it.

Last night I tried to call my son. When Terry answered the phone she refused to put him on. She insisted I speak to her before she would hand the phone over. After a little discussion and a raising in the level of voices I hung up.

I called back about half an hour later and asked again to speak to him. She refused to give him the phone until I spoke to her. Again, after a discussion and disagreement, I could not get my points across and hung up.

Later that night he called me. In the background as we spoke

I heard Terry say, "If your dad loved you, he would come back to me." Over and over again this barrage occurred. She would retort, "He doesn't F_ing love you. He should end this and come back to me." As I felt his little heart breaking apart and heard his speech cracking I knew the words were sharp and striking blows. I could hear him sob and just pray for peace as do I.

It is easy for others to stand away and judge situations and cast beliefs. It does not reflect on your everyday efforts to try to create a life out of this existence and support those you love. The police, judges and all other associated personnel don't seem to fathom the damage done by delays, rescheduling and proceedings.

I have had to walk out of the past mire and try with every bit of strength that I could find to establish a life. I do not ask for any special favors. I only would like justice to prevail for the sake of a child who can't legally fight for himself.

I am not the best parent in the world. I do, however, know that the use a child for selfish gain does not constitute loving, caring behavior. I never tell him that his mom doesn't love him. That isn't true. I ask him to make up his own mind on things he is more than capable to analyze.

I will go to the police again today and speak to them about this situation. I suspect they will say she still isn't violating her restraining order. No matter the outcome I will still stand here and fight for the freedom of spirit of a caged soul. It doesn't matter what you essentially think of me. It only matters that I go back for more every day to defend; he can not defend himself.

In closing consider this . . .

How many guys would go through the things I have seen, raise their kids and save themselves and the kids and stand?

How many guys would leave and take their kids with them?

How many guys would go into court and seek, with all of the resources they can muster, their own kids?

How many guys would drive those kids to and from school every day to keep some resemblance of the child's life intact?

I hug him and tell him I love him every day because that is what gives him the strength to get through what no child should have to face.

I guess that is why I don't always understand WHY things are the way they are.

Is anybody there? Does anybody care? Does anybody see what I see?

I would keep daily notes on the happenings and events. This is just a small sample of recordings.

However, they give you an idea of the scope of these things.

Sample Notes from My Journal:

I tried to give Terry a check for my share of the assessment. She ripped it up, threw it back at me (I have it in a bag) and then she threw my glasses. They broke. She apologized and tried to fix them. Today she asked for the check again. I told her Wednesday I'd give it to her. She was mad because I wouldn't come back. She keeps telling me that I can end this.

Terry was supposed to keep him until tomorrow night but called me and asked if I would pick him up early. I have him more than her. She constantly puts him in the middle and it is torture in my eyes. She always says he wants us together and gets him crying. I try to tell her we are adults and putting him in the middle hurts him. She says ask him what he wants. She won't listen. He gets so upset and it takes a while for him to calm down. My oldest was standing there silently.

Special note: When I dropped him off he was bathed and in clean clothes. When I picked him up today, He was still in the same clothes and had not taken a bath. That was three days. I asked him if he changed clothes. He said they were the same clothes. He also said he had not had a bath in a while.

The psychologist wants me to call to discuss working out arrangements for schools for now. I will drive him there on days when I have him. I will do what I can.

I dropped him off as scheduled. When I was there Terry paid more attention to me than him. I informed her that it was her time with him and I was leaving. She took my car keys and asked me to stay permanently. He was very affectionate and hugged me a number of times. I went inside the house and talked with Terry.

Terry told him to watch TV or play video games. He went outside and played. He prefers the quiet anyway. A little while later he came into the living room and sat Terry on the couch. He sat me on the love seat. He then came over to me and laid down and put his head on my lap and pulled a blanket over himself. There are times when the actions of a child ring true and clear. I hate all of this.

Keeping his stress to a minimum is my greatest priority. I just want him to come through this with as little permanent damage as possible. He asked how many days he had to stay with his mom. I told him a couple and I would pick him up soon. He said he hated his babysitter.

I picked him up late. I was supposed to get him at six.

They showed up and he was sun burnt. Terry said he put lotion on himself. He was burned on his face and arms and back. I had to address the sunburn that night.

Terry hollered at me because I wouldn't end things and go back to her. She said I was heartless and cruel and mean. She called me a few other things in front of our child (jerk off, heartless bastard, etc.). She wouldn't let me leave the parking lot for over half an hour. She wouldn't let me close the door and leave. She said she wanted a conjugal visit. I told her to stop and let me go. She said everything was my fault and I never tried to make things work. I fed him when I got home around eight thirty. He hadn't eaten and was hungry.

He said he hadn't bath since I dropped him off. He had just changed clothes that morning. He wore the same clothes I dropped him off in until just then, which was two days.

Terry called at least eight times to ask if I would go on a date with her. She kept insisting on meeting. I stopped answering the phone. About 9:30 PM my son answered it and after 30 minutes of her telling me she was going to go out and find another guy because we weren't married any more, I hung up.

When I went to pick up our child he started to gather toys to bring. Terry became very cross and dumped them out onto the floor. She shouted, "You cannot take anything else out of this house." Our child walked away almost in tears. I told her one truck wouldn't hurt. She said no. Instead he got to carry a box of clothes for his brother. I felt sad for him but an argument would have made it worse.

When we arrived at my house I instructed his brother to go into the attic and get trucks in boxes that I had stored there. I gave them to him and he put the boxes in his closet. He was very happy again.

Terry also informed me that if I don't come back she will get very nasty. I believe she means it. She told me how she couldn't do this. She has every intent to make things about as miserable as possible for me.

I picked up our child. He has not had a bath since I dropped him off three days ago. Terry even said he stinks. He was happy to come with me. He was till wearing the same clothes I dropped him off in.

Terry keeps insisting that the separation is over. She demands I move back in with her. When I said no, she jumped in the back of my car and wouldn't get out. She then said she wanted to come with us to the other house. I asked her to get out of the car several times. I then told her I will take the truck. She said you can't have our child then. I told her you had him last weekend. It is my weekend with him. She is now telling me how she can't handle things. All I know is I am healing and moving back in with her is not an option. I rather spend the rest of my life alone then that . . .

I was playing basketball and Terry wanted to come by the house. I told her no. Anyway she showed up and wanted to enter the house. I said no. I told her to go home. She refused. She wanted to see all of us. She then sat in the back yard with our child for a while. I wouldn't let her in my place. I was polite but firm. She was there calling me asking for ten minutes to talk. We talked for a while but she wanted more. I sent her home.

Right before she left she threatened to take my car . . . I think a restraining order should be enforced.

Phone calls I make to talk to my son have always been a real bother. She always picks up an extension and chimes in to all of our conversations. He is very reserved and walks away from the phone when she does this. However, I never pick up extensions and listen in at my house. He knows what she does is wrong. He doesn't like it either.

I ask politely to talk to him every night that she has him. She refuses to put him on until she lectures me and tells me what she wants. I have to hang up and wait for her to let him call me back. When she calls my house I put our child right on the line. Fair is not always fair, is it?

She insisted we go out on a date for our wedding anniversary. She said, "We're still married. You are my husband. You don't honor your wedding vows. I know you love me.

I can't do this anymore. THIS IS NOT WHAT I WANT! Our children want us together."

When I called last night I had a very hard time speaking to him. Terry would not allow me to talk to him. She wanted to know when I was terminating the restraining order. When she finally put him on the phone, he wouldn't talk to me because she was on another extension chiming in and throwing out comments. I hate the fact I can't even talk to my own kid.

I went over to pick our child up in the morning. I waited in the yard for him. Terry shouted things out to me and I told her to leave me alone. She then called me on my cell phone when I was in the back of the yard. I told her to stop. She chased me out into the woods behind the house to get a hug. I told her to get away. She kept walking toward me for a few minutes. I kept my distance. Finally she stopped and left for work. I could have called the police but didn't. Later that night she called my sister-in-law and told her she called me on the cell phone. She said, "I was bad. I called him on his cell phone."

Every night I ask to speak to our child numerous times. Eventually when I ignore her pleas to come over the house, she puts him on. I have learned to keep my conversation with him short and nondescript. Usually Terry is listening on the other extension and chimes in.

All of this is wearing me out . . . . . .

Lack of Education

One of the biggest problems that I have encountered when dealing with mental illness is the lack of education. In health classes all across the country they speak of many topics including sexual education, hygiene, brushing your teeth and taking a shower. There is no mention of some other problems, though. The list that I think should be touched upon includes substance abuse (drugs and alcohol), mental illness, and finally sexual abuse.

I am not saying that emphasis should be placed on just stopping problems with our kids. I am saying we should make kids aware of these problems and teach them the symptoms. Going through high school with the added knowledge of diseases such as these may stop family problems before they proceed to the next generation.

Preventative Measures

More than likely you will not be able to catch the problem before the children walk into the classroom. Maybe, though, you can make them aware of issues. Then they can stop situations from occurring with their younger brothers or sisters. Possibly they can take the knowledge home and start the recovery of other family members, including their parents.

To distinguish problems and make the appropriate authorities aware may save a family or child. If I had known before what I know now, I would have approached many things differently. Certain things that have occurred may have never happened. This is where education and knowledge can stem the tide of these things.

When you are living in these environments, you are not aware of problems. I have seen different things myself. Especially about how other families behaved. I observed certain problems and situations that I knew of. To empower the children and give them the tools to make a difference and correct problems is crucial to overcoming the problems with these situations.

To those of you who have never had to deal with these things, you have no knowledge of the everyday events and trials. Once enveloped in these things, it is often very difficult to end them, the added problem usually being that those entangled by this have no idea that anything is actually wrong.

As a child, I had no idea that there were problems. Once I reached adulthood, I learned differently. By then, though, it was too late. That is why I think it critical and necessary for the prevention of these things. Education and learning for our children is the first step to reducing these problems.

DEALING WITH ISSUES AND SUPPORT

In an ideal world "Support" is just a phone call away. That is usually not the case. I myself have called for help and been ignored. When this happens you learn to just not ask for help and deal with the crisis in front of you. Basically, you have no choice. There is nothing worse than being turned away in the middle of problems for any number of reasons by an agency that you were referred to. The sinking helpless feeling that engulfs you is strangling.

In the middle of things you never concern yourself with minor details. After all, you are just trying to keep your family safe. That can be nerve racking. Details are the least of your worries. I have seen my wife rip phones out of the wall and throw them out of windows. Yet you stand there and are asked questions. I was on the phone with a counselor. I was asked if I felt threatened or in danger by events. I replied, "Not if I go running out the door right now. I have kids, though. Do you still want her social security number?"

That and more has happened over the years. Don't let anyone tell you different. Things have gotten better, but as with any system, there is still work to be done. Luckily, I have needed help less as time went on. I learned how to handle and take care of things. This was good from the systematic viewpoint. It was just bad for me.

Going It Alone, Not a Good Idea

As the frustration mounts, there are times when your search for help becomes tedious at best. You start to give up and decide to just go it alone. That is the worst thing you can do at any time. The support and assistance of others is especially crucial in these time periods. You must always look for help.

Even though the temptation is there not to say anything to anyone, you must. Embarrassment is usually not called for. In dealing with these things, most people are very sympathetic to those family members coping with situations. Generally speaking you have done nothing wrong short of trying to support a loved one during trying times. This is not something to be ashamed of.

I spoke to family members during situations. Most have no idea how to cope and handle things. It is not lack of concern, but more lack of knowledge of handling matters of this magnitude. After many years and many situations, you find how things don't bother you as much. You learn how to make quick decisions and constantly react to ever-changing situations. Self-reliance sets in.

Although experts tell you to seek help, aid and support, these commodities are not necessarily in large supply. The ability to make contacts and seek aid may be greatly restricted when handling matters. The lack of sleep and food also play into it.

After many days and countless hours, your last thoughts are about making phone calls. When time is found, you try to get in touch with help. When you are greeted by bureaucratic red tape, your patience fades quickly and you find yourself giving up far too fast.

It is best to set up a very simple process where you only need to make one phone call to someone outside of the residence to start the alert process to the authorities. Hopefully that individual can make the calls and not be tied down by household events. That is the method that I have found works the best. If nothing else, this also adds a degree of comfort to the caretaker.

During severe episodes, phone calls out of the home were impossible. That is because all phones were removed. That pretty much eliminates the possibility. I have been questioned who I was on the phone with and what I was talking about. The paranoia that enters the mind can be overwhelming and powerful. Never underestimate it.

That is why the one-call method is the most effective, even if you have to run over to a neighbor's house to initiate it. However you can pull it off, do it. Once it is initiated, you can deal with the problems at hand and await help.

Out with the Old

As events have unfolded, I have seen many changes. These things have affected Terry, as well as me. It is impossible to experience all of this and not be affected in some way. All things evolve and change in life. Drastic events, though, change things drastically.

Personality Changes

As we get older we change. As life's events affect us we change. As we affect each other we change. These things are timeless. The way you are today and the way you will be tomorrow are slightly different. All of our experiences adjust us slightly everyday.

Through the course of things I have seen Terry's personality change. Who she was and who she is now are two different people. Some of that can be attributed to the natural course of life. Some of it, though, is due to events as written here.

I remember her spirit and confidence of old. She amazed me many a time in the way she handled herself and the way she handled me. I actually missed that. I remember her take charge, go-getter attitude and spunk. I adored her so much for it.

Now she is not so sure. She sways back and forth with indecision. She only takes a step after she looks both ways down the street and then asks if it is okay. Many a time I ask her to make up her mind. She can't. I make the decision for her. I don't like it. I miss the old days.

One Mind, Two Faces

As I have seen her change, I wonder what she is thinking. It is hard to imagine the degree of uncertainty that she has. I know that she remembers very little of the events. The split personalities that she has demonstrated are frightening. If you ever have seen the eyes of a truly deranged person, you know what the face of insanity really is. To deal with these things is beyond words.

The worst time that she demonstrated a split personality was a few years ago. One moment she was relatively calm. She was talkative and generally pleasant. She turned her head away from me. Her facial expression changed completely. She turned her head again and looked right at me. She looked right through me, as if I weren't there.

The voice inflections were completely different. Her tone also changed drastically. It appeared as if an entirely different person entered her body in an instant. She did not recognize me. She looked at me as if I were a stranger in her house. I was taken aback. I was unsure of what I was looking at.

Her mannerisms were not normal for her. She had entirely different hand and facial expressions. Her temperament was of a different degree. Her actions and reactions were much sharper and not as subtle. This was a person that I did not like at all.

Although she tolerated me, I felt out of place. She went on like this for about half an hour. We spoke to each other, but not in our usual fashion. It was as if I was a visitor in her domain. I felt a shiver run down my spine, literally.

After a while, she turned away and reverted back to herself. It was a bizarre experience. I had seen her do this before, but the previous time was not as intense. The psychiatrist had seen her do this once. He asked me if anything had triggered it. Nothing had occurred to my knowledge to cause this. She has not done it since. I would rather not see this again, ever.

When I questioned her about it she had no memory of it. She did not recall her actions. In fact, she recalled nothing that had occurred that entire day. It was one of the worst days that I can personally recall. I was glad when she came out of it and returned to relative normalcy.

Most things that have occurred I can at least deal with. The split personality issue freaks me out, though. It is hard to imagine someone that you know becoming someone else instantly. It is very hard to grasp and even harder still to deal with. It is the one area that I avoid entirely. The thought of it happening again is always in the back of my mind. Luckily, though, it hasn't.

Trust Evaporates

A sad aspect of time is the erosion of trust between us. I have seen her over time trust me less. With all of the events and occurrences, she believes that I have not always done what she feels is best. This is judged upon what she recalls of the events. I have always tried to do what was right and in her best interest. However, she has never perceived it that way.

If for any reason she has been hospitalized or treated, she believes that I failed to protect her. No matter the circumstances or chain of events, it has been perceived as my fault. In her mind I failed to protect her. I did not ensure that her rights were upheld. I failed in my duties as a husband.

To be honest, this is the one tropic that strikes me right in the heart. At all times I did what I could for her. In fact, many times I personally sacrificed on her behalf and she never knew it. I always felt that it was my duty to do what had to be done, no matter what the cost. It really hurt me the first time she told me that she didn't trust me. I never forgot her saying that to me. I know that she may not have meant it. It still hurt me deeply, though.

Through all of these things I always maintained a higher standard for myself on her behalf. I never once swayed from that. I did what could be done under the most severe of circumstances. I often wonder if I could have done more. At the time, though, I didn't know what I could do. Those of us who go through these things often regret not doing more. We may not know what we could have done, but we wonder if we did enough.

It is not that we feel guilt for these things. It is more that we feel helpless. The events as they take place rule our lives and we struggle and strain to aid and assist as we can.

There are times, though, with all of our efforts, we are lost. There is no manual or script that can be followed. There are only signs and symptoms that are to be watched and waited upon.

What Happened to My Best Friend

As the years passed I always wondered one thing: What happened to my best friend? I guess not too many guys think that way. I always felt Terry was my best friend. As things happened, though, I realized that maybe she wasn't. It was a sad day when that happened. After all that we had been through, she was no longer at the place she had held before with me. It took me a while to come to terms with it.

It was the equivalent of seeing your favorite dog die. It may even be as bad as watching your best fishing rod sink to the bottom of the lake. Worse yet, it was like watching the shotgun your grandfather gave you drop out of the tree and over the cliff, never to be seen again.

As I started to heal, I wondered why she questioned me going to therapy. I had hoped that she would support me and help. I found that she didn't want any part of my healing. She felt threatened by it. I, on the other hand, just wanted to get better.

After many years of marriage, it is not easy to separate yourself from your wife. I, in an instant, had to. If I was to heal, I had to do it alone. I felt sad at the thought that it might cost me my marriage. On the other hand, if I didn't do it, I would never be right. For the first time in my life, I became selfish.

When you are with someone for so long, you never think about the fact that you are separate. You each have choices and decisions that must be made every day. To make decisions as a couple becomes a natural response. You instinctively consider each other's points of view and decide accordingly. To break yourself of this habit and just consider your own best interest is a lot harder then you might think.

This is a whole new concept to someone who is codependent. I have to force myself to think that way. To sacrifice for the good of others has always been the way. Not to do it is very difficult. My own needs have always come last and were rarely if ever considered. As I get better at thinking and deciding for myself, Terry has called me arrogant. I am not any such thing. I just don't put everyone else before my own basic needs now.

I am setting boundaries and limits that all must follow. I am saying no. I am starting to define myself. Since Terry was no longer my best friend, I found that I must be my own best friend. It is long overdue. In all the commotion I lost touch with that person. It will take me a while to find that person in me again.

Does Age Bring Peace?

It is interesting to note that psychiatrists have told me that as time goes on, the problem may go away. I find this to be a fascinating fact. It is amazing to me how the mind, over time, can work out these kinds of issues and dispense of them.

I guess with age comes tolerance. Could it be caused by the lack of immediate recall? Past emotional events possibly get buried deeper with age. Therefore, we have fewer reactions to similar situations. The human mind is a wonderful instrument but it to lacks some capabilities. Like a computer hard drive, it has a working capacity limit that, once reached, makes thought reprocessing much more difficult. Memories and other such events are stored away, but as we get older, they become harder to retrieve.

I find that although I know things, the time that it takes to remember specific details is delayed. It sometimes drives you crazy. You know something. It is on the tip of your tongue, but it takes a minute to come up with. Could this be a protective measure in our genetic makeup? Who knows?

REFLECTIONS

As I look back over many years of things I have come to a realization. All of the things that I have seen and done in my life are tied together in one long, twisted stretch, like rope. Each individual act tied to all others acts before and after it in some way. This creates a series that carries on until cut or broken by some force.

I have always maintained that the events with Terry were self-inclusive. There was never any thought to there being a cause of things before that began. I now look back and see that there was. For me, this all started many years before I met Terry. It is interesting how I find connections that I never thought possible.

ALCOHOLISM AND CODEPENDENCY

The harder that I look at things, the more I see where this all began for me. I was raised in a house with alcoholics. I didn't know any better. At age 4, I would be able to drink beer or wine from a glass, if I went to the refrigerator to refill it. This was normal behavior to me. Two six packs a day were what every parent drank, right?

This went on until much later in my life. By the time that I realized this was wrong it was too late. I had already been introduced into the world of codependency. This term I am learning well. I have been a prisoner of it since I was about 4 or 5. If you grow up looking after others during their afflictions, you may become codependent. These series of events began for me a long road with this syndrome.

The good news here is that when I realized it was wrong I would not drink. I currently only have a glass of wine on very few occasions. I often go years without drinking at all. I have far too many memories associated with alcohol, very few of them good.

I remember being about 5. I did something wrong. I can't remember what it was. I remember my father hitting me with a television antenna on the legs. He usually used a belt. On this day, though, he opted for the antenna. I remember the marks that it left. For days that summer I had to wear long pants to hide them. I was so ashamed.

The welts lasted for over a week. The pain lasted a lot longer. I wish I knew what I had done. I only wonder if it was all that bad. I remember being hit up until I was about 13. That was the last time that I remember.

I wanted my father to stop drinking. My mother said he was an alcoholic. We would count the beers every morning. It was usually around 12. I remember one time hiding his beer. I paid dearly for that. I never hid his beer again.

If you put your hand in his bag of potato chips while he was drinking, you took your life in your hands. That was a big mistake. I remember friends asking if they could have some. I told them I wouldn't do that. It is the equivalent of putting your arm down a crocodile's mouth.

Often, my parents would fight about the drinking. My mother was afraid to call him an alcoholic, even though she knew he was. My father would stay up until 12:30 every night. He would go to bed and I would hear my mother scold him. He didn't care. He had his beer. He was okay for another day. That is how it went for many years.

The worst thing that I did was to pour his booze down the sink one day. I was just fed up and I poured every bottle that I could find. He was so mad at me. However, my mother stepped in. To my knowledge he never hit her. That time, he came close.

When I got older he said it was okay to drink, as long as we never left the house. I guess this was a controlled form of the disease. Keep it in the house and family. Don't go outside with it. As a kid, this was okay with me. I see the error in those ways now.

Wine Maker

The one thing that my father always enjoyed was making his own wine. After many years he became quite good at it. He developed a talent for it. Every year he would proceed to gather the ingredients and concoct a batch of wine.

After the fermentation process was complete he would proudly announce that the liquid was ready for consumption. This was probably the one time that we as teenagers were hesitant to drink alcohol. Certain years and types of wine that he made could be construed as dangerous chemicals.

If you just wanted to get drunk, then they were perfect. If however you wanted to keep your sanity after drinking it, then you most assuredly thought about it. Rocket fuel was generally the term that we applied to some of his elixirs. One year he made extra and the fluid sat in a container until the next year. It took a lot of courage to get up the nerve to try it. I was actually shocked that the bottle held it for that long.

If You Got 'Em Smoke 'Em

I remember trying to alter his cigarettes and cigars. I would put paper clips in them trying to get him to stop. I sprinkled pepper on them, dipped them in hot sauce, and anything else that I could think of. Usually, it just ended up with me being punished. I figured that I deserved it. I was trying to do the right thing in the wrong way. None my antics ever worked.

Every night I would go to bed up the steps from the living room. I remember hating it. As I went up the steps I had to pass through the barrier of smoke that always existed. About 18 inches to 2 feet down from the ceiling was this layer of smoke. In order to pass through it you had to hold your breath and run up the steps.

The one thing that I always hated was being sent to the store to buy more cigarettes. This really bothered me. I felt guilty for being a contributing factor in the problems. I couldn't say no. I had to do it. I tried to get a list of other things that I could buy. I would ask about bread, milk, butter, or anything else to give the trip purpose. Then the cigarettes were just a small part.

Growing Pains

As I grew older, I never fit in. I kept to myself and decided that I did not belong. I could never explain why I had these feelings. I just felt inferior. I had a hard time with relationships. Friends were hard to make and keep. It seemed that I never rated. They were always better then me. I grew tired of this.

When I started dating it was really difficult. I wouldn't think of asking out the pretty girls. There was no way they would lower themselves to my level. After a few years I found Terry. We seemed to get along, possibly because her family had various problems that resembled my family's issues. Maybe that was the common ground we found. We clicked.

After we dated for a while, we fell in love and got married. It was fine for a few years. Then the past caught up to us. At first, I had no idea what was going on. As things happened I learned. It was odd how I dealt with her problems. It was like getting back in the saddle. I never understood why I could do things that no one else would even think of. Now I know why. I grew up learning all about how to be codependent. I had been tuning my craft since day one.

It is only now that I realized that something was wrong. It took a friend to tell me how dysfunctional my life was. I never knew it. Now, though, I am trying to correct it. Maybe with any luck, I can fix this. We'll see.

I listen now to other people's stories and problems. It strikes me how I am not the only one with these issues. I always felt alone. I know now that I am not. I don't revel in others' stories, but just to hear those makes you think that maybe it is okay to have these problems and try to deal with them. Maybe there is not something fundamentally wrong with yourself that all others were created okay and you weren't. It is somewhat comforting to find that you are a human being with problems, but you are okay.

Childhood Thoughts

I was a solitary child. I read a lot and played only with a few friends. I never really sought out other people. I was shy and introverted. In school I kept to myself and never figured on others wanting me to participate.

Although I played sports I never thought I was any good. In high school I was a captain although I really didn't want the position. Sports banquets and such bothered me. To receive trophies or awards was difficult. I hated large groups and preferred small gatherings.

Speaking in front of the class was always a chore. I only completed the tasks necessary for the topic or class. In high school I was informed of my writing abilities and wrote speeches and announcement addresses. To hear anything I wrote over the loud speaker really bothered me. I would try to find an excuse to go outside when I knew they would read something.

The only advantage to being relatively solitary was my imagination. I constantly improved on that aspect. I could create and fabricate ideas and games with no trouble. I used to play and build and exercise my mind. Although not in an orthodox way, it was very entertaining.

I never liked television as much as reading. I could use everyday items to amuse myself. Even now with writing I practice by taking a simple object and writing about it. It is a very good training exercise.

I always found that one can learn a great deal by steady and concentrated observation of all things around him. I practiced that from an early age. It gave me the benefit of seeing before any words were spoken.

I always knew that just because you were quiet didn't mean you had nothing to say. Actually I found that those who were quieter had volumes to speak. Sometimes they just didn't see the point considering who was around them. I was guilty of that.

Animals only speak when they have something real to say. Why can't people be more like that?

I always wondered why if we are so evolved why we forgot the art of listening.

Why Tell You this?

That is a very good question. The answer is this: You have to understand where I came from in order to understand why things happened the way they did. As with anyone's life, things don't occur without reason. All actions and reactions that occur are based on the past in some way or form.

It also gives you an understanding as to why I have the ability to stand here and tell you something. If I give an opinion it is based on all I have seen and endured. It is hard for anyone who has not endured such things to understand. However, you would be surprised at how many actually do experience such things daily and refuse or can't recognize it.

I am not an expert in these matters and do not profess a doctorial stance. However, in enduring such things for years I have found that academic text books leave out the truth that only those who have seen it first hand realize.

In our everyday existence there is only one person who is ultimately responsible for our actions. You can try to blame others or convince yourself that it was because of others' actions that things occurred. The truth is you are the one who is solely responsible for the outcome in most if not all matters.

Why did I not continue with these things? Well, I knew in my heart of hearts that it was wrong. I knew that for my sake and my kids I had to get out. I could no longer allow others to dictate what I should do and when. I had to walk the walk.

Was it easy? Of course it wasn't. It was long and tearful and brutal and demanding. Yet somehow, someway, I managed to do it. With no regrets I sit here and write the story. Sometimes the little guy who has all the odds against him wins.

How does that happen? Well for no other reason than because in each of us there is a person who is strong and willing and able to do what must be done. No glory, no medals, no parades. Just stand up and do what you believe is right no matter the odds or outcome.

"When inner strength is all that you have left, it can be the most powerful weapon anyone could ever imagine!"

The Beginning

"Judge me not by my methods or the course I
take. Consider the weight of the load.
For others cannot understand the task.
Given to one who is able."

Where to Begin?

My wedding day. I thought that day was the best day I would ever know. I found out it would begin for me a lesson I would never forget. When you get married you think it is forever and you love the other person with all of your heart and soul. You would never think of "harming" them and hope they would never think of "harming" you.

Let's think about that for a second. What is harm? It can be a physical, it can be mental, or it can be emotional. It can be a punch or slap. It can be with harsh and cruel words. It can be when nothing is said or no physical violence is done. It can be simply the lack of support given to each other through trying times. All of these things and more add up to abuse in one form or another.

They are all horrific in their own ways. Physical harm tends to leave visible marks and sometimes emotional pain. The greatest form to me, though, is the mental and emotional abuse of someone else. The abuse created when they are thinking they love you, but in essence are torturing, using and controlling you. It is an abuse without visual scars but very emotional ones. It does not bleed red. It bleeds clear with many tears. It becomes a much deeper and longer lasting injury.

The problem is neither of you may realize it is sometimes being done. That is what makes it a brutal injury. It is an unintentional form of torture. When you add a mental illness, of any variety, to the mix along with everyday trials of marital life, you have a formula for a nightmare. The institution of marriage can be a breeding ground for such a situation. Whether intentional or not, it happens.

At the wedding, you take your vows and promise to love, honor and cherish your new lifelong partner. You are in love and your vision is clouded and warped by your hopes and dreams of a future happy life together. You may or may not have been involved to that level before and you would do almost anything for that person. Love is not blind, but it is visually impaired. You usually know romance and a loving caress. The realities of living together under all circumstances and dealing with each other's pasts are still just whims. Soon, however, they will become a full frontal assault of epic proportion.

But didn't I say for better or worse, in sickness and in health? So you wait for the better not the worse and in health not in sickness portions to take over and be patient. You believe in your heart and mind that they will come.

Wedding Day

Feb 4

Music plays, all await motions that are so dear.
Pews are filled, family and friends, anticipate event of year.
Nerves are strained and feast is set to delight and entertain.
Dressed and prompted for every move. Waiting acts to gain.

Stanza changes, congregation will rise to see the walk of life.
It changes for the rest of time the essence of the wife.
Slow and sure, arms locked around, a tear will form and hide.
For father takes the last of strides to give away the bride.

A shake of hands and gentle kiss do signal departing girl.
A turn with stand as set for life. A woman draped in pearl.
Now come the words and gentle voice of holiest intent.
Thoughts with nods, a hopeful phrase through which the day is sent.

The beauty comes from not just look but act of solemn show.
To tell the world their love shall bond and for the rest will grow.
Old words can not define the nights long on winter eves.
Displayed the effort seen on minds, but in God's hands reprieve.

A ring and veil and promise made, they stand and beam with glows.
"I now pronounce" are leading words a married couple knows.
A kiss with hug, seal the pact, the future waits in wing.
It marches forth yet seals the heart with music that shall sing.

Wedding Day begins the course that marriage will endure.
It casts off lines of olden bonds and turns the heart so pure.
Remember that the trials faced will surely tax the bride.
This day of party only starts the walk you take with pride.

Actions come to tear apart the bonds set here in stone.
Forgive the acts and love with soul to keep the joining known.

Age and time will never break the grip that love has secured.
It holds on fast to all events and leads through paths endured.

In many years with children grown you look back and wonder why.
It makes you think and makes you laugh and eventually you will cry.
Memories that begin this day and will last throughout your life.
With kiss and nod and loving touch you become this day a wife.

You live this day hopefully to repeat the process once again.
In many years as mother of the white-clad girl you send.
She will grow like you and stand in view. Measured by her Mom.
Pride and love will hold her close and give her look of Prom.

When all is said and sun is set your life shall carry forth.
A photo album will bring back joys and speak of this day's worth.
Keep close the love and best felt times, for time will carry past.
As age crawls by its wisdom comes. Your children make it last.

The First Episode

Things were fine in our marriage for about five years. This is when a radical behavior change occurred. The initial happenings were dismissed by me as her just being annoyed or angered at something that I had done. Even though I couldn't figure out what it was, I thought maybe it was something I had forgotten. I had known her since we were both very young. I had not seen any radical behavior from her or major mood swings before. I was about to be schooled on the meaning of Dementia, Paranoia, Bi-polar and Stress Disorder tendencies.

Class Begins

You have no idea of the degree of rage that an individual can exhibit. Docile people can turn into raving lunatics. When someone looks right through you with assumed hate and evil in their eyes, especially a loved one, you wonder what capabilities man really has. The first time that she looked right through me, I wondered who this person was. Billy Joel sings a song about someone with "the face of a stranger." This is exactly who I was dealing with one morning. Unknown to me, it was the time of year. It would take me another 14 years to figure out what was the catalyst. For the moment, I just decided to deal, hang on and ride it out.

Episodes are usually very frightening experiences for those who are not accustomed to it. Periods such as this are generally triggered. She was not feeling well. She had a fever. It had triggered inner feelings that she had secured away. Other triggering mechanisms may be a smell or sound similar to ones experienced at the time of incidents. It is often very hard to determine. Once triggered, medication, time and counseling are your only allies.

In the next two weeks I saw a rapid progression of anger, rage, hatred and overall intolerance for anyone. She became extremely argumentative and at times, violent. Her sleep habits changed drastically as well. She went from her normal sleep of about seven hours daily to about twenty minutes a day. I tried my best to stay awake and keep her out of trouble, but it became too much for me. Most people don't realize that someone suffering from mental illness can exist on minimal sleep and food for extended periods of time. She would often disappear into the night and wander. I would look for her to no avail. She would show up again the next morning.

I was worried, frightened and unsure of what to do. Family support was non-existent. They scattered like mice at her rage and anger and left me to bare the brunt. I could not leave our son. My work suffered and I struggled to keep a rapidly crumbly house intact. This first episode went on for about 6–8 weeks. At the end I tried to piece back the house and contents. I received paperwork, clothes, and other belongings from neighbors for weeks after its finish. To this day certain items were never recovered and I have given them up for being lost.

At a counselors suggestion I called Crisis Intervention. The individual listened to my story and asked if I could put Terry on the phone. I gladly handed the phone to her. She spoke a few choice words, ripped the phone cord out of wall and threw the phone and cord out of the window. I called them back and informed them that all further requests for her should be submitted in writing. The counselor did not laugh.

So it went on for another four weeks and I tried to no avail to get help. If and when I could get her to go to counseling by whatever means I could come up with, she would argue, holler and generally throw fits of rage. The counselors said that she had an anger management problem.

Eventually the lack of sleep and food caught up with her. She began to feel sick. She began sleeping more. She slowly reverted back to her old self and in time, remembered nothing. I was puzzled and unsure of what had happened. But I was glad that the ordeal was finally over. Little did I know that this was only the first round.

You would think that when it was over, family would come back and offer assistance. You are wrong. It is amazing how they want to know your business until this kind of trouble is involved. I struggled to put the house back in order. Terry said she did a pretty good job at spring cleaning. This would be her mantra. From here on out, it would send a cold shiver down my spine.

Psychiatrists have told me that this behavior is common. Later I understood what was happening. In the beginning, though, I had no clue.

UNWANTED GUEST

The scariest event of this episode occurred when I woke up at around 2:00 AM to find Terry in the living room of our house. In the shadows in a corner, I saw the figure of a man. I did not know who it was, nor did I care. My child was about 20 feet from me in the bedroom sleeping and I was determined to protect him. I ordered the person out of the house immediately.

The man mumbled a few words about being friends with Terry, and then left abruptly. To this day I do not know who that individual was. Terry says she knew him. All that I can tell you is that I have not seen this individual again. I do not know how he ended up in my house. Just the thought of what might have happened has given me the chills.

Shortly after that, Terry left abruptly as well and drove away in our truck. She showed up the next day without the vehicle. The police called me a while later. They had found our truck at a lake about four miles away.

Later that day, I had a neighbor drive me to the truck. Upon close inspection I found nothing wrong or missing. I drove the truck back home. Why she left it there, I will never know. She doesn't remember leaving it.

END OF THE BEGINNING

So ended the first episode. It is odd for you to hear this, but it was tame by later standards. It was a learning experience for me. It was the start of a series of events that has gone on until today.

Many have no idea of the scope of these things. To get through these events with everyone healthy and reasonably safe is a blessing. At the time, though, I thought my world was coming to an end. I look back now and almost laugh at it. It was no more than a minor speed bump.

As things have happened over the years I have learned

to put things into perspective. Things would get much worse as I would soon learn. This was assuredly the least severe full episode that I have encountered to date.

That is what makes this existence such a contrast from reality. You learn how to deal and cope with it to the point of considering it normal behavior. You expect it from others and eventually yourself. That is part of the sickness that invades your entire life. Could you imagine considering this normal? Many do that every day.

Initial Feelings

To be honest all that I could think about was that it was over. We had fared well and had gotten through the entire fiasco. Not knowing what was happening, I just wanted it to end. When it had run its course, I sat back and took a deep breath. Although I didn't understand a bit of it, I was just relieved. I brushed myself off and continued on with things. I thought possibly something had bothered her. Maybe now she got it out of her system.

Things seem to return to normal and I let the whole bad event slip into memory. That is, until it happened again. When I saw it could happen any year, then I began to question what was going on. At this point, what do you do? We had attended marriage counseling before. It didn't seem like she was angry at me. Something was bothering her, though.

Close My Eyes

13 Oct

Some mornings I just close my eyes as I walk down the street.
I would rather not see, all of the things that I do meet.

If blindness of thought could rule my world, a peace would follow so. But vision is what vision is, and sight is what I know.

Others look yet never see. A cloud will block their view.
Haziness envelopes them. God has shielded them true.
The chosen few with clear eyes have tears hidden so.
The clarity is the worst of it, the sharpness don't you know.

A blurry looking keyboard can always be a friend.
The keystrokes are so soothing as if meaning has an end.
My thoughts and visions upon the journey never go away.
The hardest part of reality, knowing of another day.

I gave up explanations for the futility of the act.
To talk and explain is useless, brought about by a pact.
So on we go into the realm; no one gives what's brought.
Closed-minded drones speak loud but never give a thought.

We silent ones who know the way are never asked for light.
We try our best to make it true. The effort through the night.
At dawn the sleep awake from dreams. Refreshed and enlightened so. The quiet few reflect and pause, at dawn's rebirth and glow.

So ends my tale with these words, to always think upon.
A phrase or notion of the day with hope to surely come.
Remembrance when you think past the narrow sheltered view.
For it is written, it shall be done, as God intended to.

Knee Deep In It

After the first episode things calmed down. I dismissed any thoughts of it happening again. About the same time the next year she became agitated again. It did not seem nearly as intense to me, though. We talked and made appointments for marriage counseling. We spoke to the counselors and they gave us each things to work on. I tried to deal with things as best as I could but things never seemed to get better.

She seemed angry with me. She was irritated by the least little thing and complained constantly. This was not her usual way. I visited the counselors with and without her, but it did not seem to help. She had moderate periods of anger, but never posed a threat to herself or others.

As time went on she would inform me that she needed to spring clean. She would thoroughly trash the house but proclaim she was reorganizing things. As I tried to follow her around and clean up after her, she would verbally dispense me. There were times when I was literally knee deep in it. This is not an exaggeration. She would pile everything from where she found it. I learned fast to dispense of all of the clutter that I could find. It is amazing how much stuff you actually have that you don't know about.

The paperwork problem is one of those things that does not end. All year long she has a problem. I find that I am constantly going through paperwork that she accumulates. She never throws any of it out. Magazines, ads from newspapers, mail advertisements and numerous catalogs are collected and stored. As I find them, I discard them. When I need something that came in the mail, I ask her. She will normally point me to a specific bag or box that may or may not contain the item. If it doesn't, the search is on.

When it comes in, she just puts the mail in various containers. I find it in bags, boxes, under furniture, on chairs and tables and lots of other places. Every time I open a drawer or closet, I find more. When I go into the attic to clean, I find bags and boxes full. I shred and clean them out and more appear. When she works, she brings home papers from there. Sometimes it drives me crazy. I have spent days at a time shredding and still lost ground. It can be very frustrating. One

Saturday I shredded papers from dawn till dusk. I filled eight trash bags with shredded paper.

Through a two-month episode, I would clean the house countless times. It would get so frustrating that I would just back up the truck and shovel and throw things out the door into it. I would also open a window and do the same. Many things were broken or missing parts. Don't ask. Anyway, I became good at cleaning and to this day find myself cleaning by reflex. It happens even more when I get nervous.

After a while, when I cleaned, I wouldn't even ask. I would just take care of business. Usually I'd start and eventually she would realize what I was doing. If I didn't keep it under control, it would get out of hand. I have many times gone through a room and upon finishing, found more materials hidden away.

The other thing that I do is give her a time frame. If she does not use or dispose of an item that she is saving by the end of that time frame, I will remove it. One year she picked an object that she said she wanted to repair. It had a broken frame and other damage. I knew it would be a very hard piece to repair. She said that she wanted to work on it. I waited one year and told her that if she didn't start fixing it, I would throw it out. She did nothing. At the end of the time, I backed up the truck, loaded it in, and threw it out. She never doubted my word again.

Hospitalization

During the most severe episodes I could not handle her. I tried my best, but to no avail. Eventually she would need to be institutionalized. You may think that this alleviated my stress. You are wrong. I visited her every day to assure her that she was not alone. I brought her clothes and other belongings. I brought the kids and just made the best out of it. Usually hospitalization lasted from 3 weeks to whatever was determined by the courts and doctors. When you are committed involuntarily, you wave the right to leave of your own free will.

There were times in Hospital Court that I did not know what the doctors would say. Generally, they would discuss their opinions with me and we would reach a reasonable conclusion. I defended her as best I could, but I knew she needed help to get well. As the medication, counseling and controlled environment helped, they would eventually release her. She would come home bitter and mad at me for doing this to her. I truly believe that hospitalization kept her alive.

There were interesting aspects of institutions to me. One was the fact that the level of quality of care that you receive in therapy, doctors or counselor interviews was not cost dependent. The more they cost, the better the food they served, though.

One time, when she was admitted, I was laid off. This gave me time to see her, but I did not have insurance. The only hospital that would take her was a county facility. You would think that the care given would be sub-par to a private facility. You are quite wrong.

It was actually this county facility and a remarkable doctor that finally determined what the causes were. After long therapy sessions and a lengthy stay, he determined her initial problem. At the time we thought this was a monumental breakthrough.

With this information we set out to correct a wrong and try to make it right. After her stay there, and some counseling, she did not have a severe episode for a long period. There were still things being worked on. I still saw minor occurrences. But, hopefully, the worst was in the past. After many years and countless traumatic events, maybe there was light at the end of the tunnel.

There is one major point that I would like to make here. You often do not know when mental illness will strike. You never know for how long it will subject you to its grasp. You most assuredly will never know if it will come back and greet you again. Medical conditions are generally controlled with medications. Mental illness, even with medication, will haunt you for the rest of your days. This is part of the struggle that some of us endure. You can run, but you can never hide.

Staff

One thing that always impressed me about the institutions and hospitals was the staff. Generally speaking, they had to deal with the same kinds of things that I did. I found them to be courteous and kind. It takes a special person to do that kind of work. I always admired them.

I have to honestly say that if it was not for the quality of care she received at the hospitals, I am not sure she would be around today. The counseling and therapy proved immeasurable. I never envied the staff, though. They had to deal with far more people than me, and do it every day. I, on the other hand, only had to deal with one. The only advantage that they had over me was that they went home every night. I was home.

Jig Saw Puzzles

Some of the activities at the institutions would make me jealous at times. They had arts and crafts, painting, and other games and puzzles. What I liked to do most when I was there were the jig saw puzzles. To sit down with a group of patients and actually work on a puzzle was good for me. When the kids were with Terry, I would try to help complete a puzzle. Many times I found the puzzle left in the same degree of completion and position from the day before. I realized that the patients did not care so much about the puzzle as they did spending time trying to work it out.

Other Patients

Patients at the institutions I found to be sociable, and at times entertaining. They picked on each other and joked just the same as you or me. They were much more alert and capable than you might think. Sedation may have slowed them down, but I believe their hearts were in full gear.

I usually had no trouble making friends with patients, and found very few had visitors. Some of them were jealous of Terry. I usually came daily. I noticed that a few hadn't had a visitor all year. When I would see that, I would write their name on the visitor log just to make them feel better. This would brighten their day. It really didn't matter whom I came to see, or whom I wrote. It was just the act that made them happy.

Medication

The use of medication is essential with some people. It is often used to control mood swings and allow doctors to determine problems through the therapy sessions. The few times that a family member actually visited Terry, they were appalled by her slow reactions and speech. It did not bother me at all. I was used to it. I found the better the hospital, the less medication they used on a daily basis. It is a general rule of thumb to use enough medication to control, but not to subdue.

A psychiatrist suggested a possible seasonal disorder and we approached the problems from that direction. He suggested medication for that period of time, but she refused it. I on the other hand gladly accepted, but he would not give it to me. This was not the only time the refusal of medication would happen. Believe me, I asked.

Every time an incident or a hospitalization occurred the suggestion of the doctors would be that she should go on a small medication. Even if it would be temporary during her anticipated episode period, she refused. I never thought that too much to ask in consideration of family.

Then again the whole problem here was that in order to be cured, you had to willfully admit something was wrong.

Warning Signs

Her episodes would come about the same time of year. Although they did not come every year, they came often enough. After a number of them I started to pick up on the warning signs. Most of the symptoms came gradually. If you did not keep an eye on her, you could miss the subtle changes and be caught off guard.

My Guide List

The following is a list of warning signs that I had seen.

1) Loss of sleep. It would gradually change from 6–7 hours a day, down to 2–3 hours or less. Twenty minutes a day was her worst period.

2) Drop off of appetite. It could go from 3 meals daily to maybe 1 snack.

3) Mood swings. These usually occurred gradually. Consider a wave on the ocean. A small wave starts out as 1 foot high at its peak, and 1 foot low at its trough. When it gets higher, 6–8 feet,

its trough gets lower. This is what happens with the mood swings. The highs get higher, almost like euphoria, and the lows get lower, like depression.

4) Random thoughts with no clear point or direction and unorganized behavior. Some of us suffer from this all of the time.

5) Paranoid tendencies. These included the belief that neighbors, the government or others were watching and plotting against her.

6) A complete lack of trust in immediate family members and friends, especially those who really were trustworthy.

7) Multiple layering of clothing. No matter what the temperature. She would not change clothes, just add to them.

8) Unkempt, unclean, or no hygiene practices.

9) Wandering with no real direction or place to go.

10) Phone calls to anyone and everyone at all hours.

11) A complete lack of ability to tell time. Day/Night was meaningless.

Battening Down the Hatches

Once I had seen enough symptoms, and I knew she was going to enter an episode, I would start taking precautionary measures. These would include the following steps as well as others. You have to understand that reducing and preventing any unnecessary damage and injury become crucial to recovery and survival. Unfortunately, these things are not taught. They are only learned through experience. Many things are done not to hurt or control, but to protect her, myself and my kids.

Precautionary Measures

1) Hide and lock away an important paperwork.

2) Cancel all credit cards except one. The one exception would be the card that only I have.

3) Remove any unnecessary cash from the household.

4) Park and disable all vehicles that I will not need.

5) Inform my work of possible problems. This I would not do until necessary.

6) Inform state or local police of current situation.

7) Call specific family members and let them know. Just in case.

8) Call doctor or counselor. Just to put them on alert.

9) Hide or remove anything in the house that might present a problem. (This includes any weapons, knives, etc . . . that I can think of)

10) Inform the kids' school. (They can look out for problems on their end)

These are some of the steps that I had to take. As various things occurred I would take more. This was my start off list. If I could not do anything else, I would take care of these. Once completed, I would monitor her progress and eliminate any and all stress that I could. With any luck, I could deal with things at home. If she became too bad, though, hospitalization was required.

KIDS AND MY COUNSELING

As things would occur, I found it necessary to make sure that the kids could, if they wanted to, talk to counselors. This they did on occasion. It was never forced upon them. To my knowledge, from talking to the counselors, things have worked out okay, though, they did express concern and at times embarrassment. It is hard for anyone to understand these things, let alone kids. When the oldest was very young, this all started. The youngest was born into this.

CALLING THE SCHOOL

At the onset of an episode I call the school and alert them. She has shown up there and caused problems in the past. It is also a good idea for them to know so they can talk to the kids while at school. If and when Terry wanders in, the school is much more likely not to overreact if they know about things beforehand.

Usually the staff is very accommodating and I have never had a problem. She has freaked out during some parent-teacher conferences. My oldest remembers one in particular when he was in sixth grade and she lost it. We ushered her out of the school and the teacher filed a report with child agencies. All was dropped after review.

Believe me when I tell you that I have had issues with state child care agencies. They have been to my house on several occasions to investigate. They have never found anything or given me a hard time. They are just doing their job. I understand this and cooperate fully. There are many aspects to these episodes that I rather not go into.

Getting Help for Myself

The problem with getting help for me has always been an issue of time. It is crucial that I resolve and handle the aspects of these events. When they are resolved, I deal with me.

I have sought counseling. There are times when I need it more then others. I have found that when quiet times occur, I recall events. These are the roughest times for me. To reflect can be very painful. I have learned to keep busy.

I have started writing and this provides me with an outlet that allows me to express myself at my own pace. Upon completion of this work, I will begin something else to vent my stress.

Professional help is usually a very good idea for people dealing with these things. I have not sought counseling enough through the years. Therapy is one of the many things that I must work on for the future.

Many a counselor has asked me how I have dealt with things through the years. The truthful answer is, I don't know. I have not been trained for these things. It is not a natural state to be in. I have just found that I do the best that I can and do not worry about the rest.

What you must realize is that these events just occur and there is really not much you can do about them. All you can do is react once they start. Just like a hurricane or tornado, they just happen.

I started therapy again recently because I felt I had to. I do not consider this a weak thing. I think actually it shows my resolve to maintain a clear, level head for dealing with matters. Terry did not have a problem with it as long as she didn't have to go. After a few sessions I am beginning to feel better about myself. I will not lie to you and tell you that there is nothing wrong. I have my own issues. Some are generated by these events. Others stem from my family and the past.

The funny thing about therapy is the more that I go, the more that I realize that I need it. I hope that it is a sign that I am getting better. Now before I go, I think about things that I want to bring up with the counselor.

The time goes fast in sessions, so the more organized I am, the better. Once we get into a session, things will take a direction. As long as I can walk away at the end with learning something about myself, it is okay. It fascinates me to figure out why I feel about things the way that I do. You never realize how events from the past mold your future.

The greatest challenge in therapy for me is communication. Telling the therapist how you feel can be very difficult. Many times I am not sure how I feel. It takes a number of questions or scenarios to figure out where I stand. Once I do it is like a light bulb going off. To realize how you feel can be uplifting and enlightening. It gives you a sense of freedom. At that point you can make a decision or a stand. The weight of things is lifted off of your shoulders.

Writing Is My Savior

As I mentioned, the greatest therapy that I have found is writing. It is often very difficult for me to express how I feel. With writing, though, I can take my time and say exactly what I mean the first time. Words on paper can be more easily juggled than in speech. That is the way that I feel. When I read back what I have written, I am often amazed. It stuns me sometimes to see how I really feel.

I find that I can express abstract thoughts easier as well. Spoken words skip over true meaning. With written words, I can precisely pinpoint what I am trying to say.

I feel better after I write as well. I especially like to go back later and see what my thoughts were on something. It sometimes surprises me how my feelings have changed drastically toward something. Over time I can see attitude changes and see my healing progress. I see little things every day. Big changes occur much more gradually.

Other people have enjoyed my writing as well. It is easier for me to hand them written words than have a conversation about a topic. Once they read things, then we discuss each other's viewpoints. This makes for an open, productive session. It also allows them to point out flaws or strengths in my opinions or viewpoints. To debate positions and compromise is much easier.

The best part of writing as a therapy is you can do it as the mood strikes you. I have found that driving down the road thoughts come to me. I jot notes down and continue when I get back home. Some days my mind never stops. I try to record what I can. The rest I just rewrite as time allows.

Golden Oldies

In going through notes I have found things that I have written a while ago. I forgot about them. I read the material and it amazes me. Some things I really like. Others I don't.

When I find things that I have written years ago, I wonder why my feelings had changed so towards it. I realize that as we grow and change, we see things differently.

Stories, poetry, and snippets are my favorites. I really like to read things that I wrote when growing up. The imagination and innocent-eyed tales of youth are refreshing. My only problem is that sometimes I don't agree with the grade that the teacher gave me. I thought it was better than that. I just shake my head now. I show some of them to the kids. They like reading old stories of mine.

They also like the old drawings and artwork that I have found. I recently came across and old painting that I did back in high school. After all of these years it still looks pretty good. I found a story that I had written back in grade school. It had an illustration with it. I was surprised when I saw it. I had forgotten all about it. I only received a B as a grade. I thought it was better than that.

My parents saved a lot of things that I wrote growing up. I am grateful for that. I look back on some nights and really enjoy the stories. Some things that I wrote were very dark. I find that many times I still write that way. It stems, I believe, from growing up in a house with an alcoholic. I am just learning that now.

Other writings that interest me now are things that my mother wrote to me. We always had a way to communicate. Although we hardly ever agreed on anything, we respected each other. Her writings now are dear to me. She knew of the difficulties involved with a father who was an alcoholic. It just never sunk into me when growing up. They mean that much more to me now when I read the letters.

Marriage Counseling

Before Episodes

Our marriage and friendship went well and there had been no need. I don't claim to be the most understanding guy, but I tried my best. We didn't fight. There were occasions that we have differences of opinions. The first few years of our marriage were fine. As we learned about each other, we grew closer. We have a lot of common interest. I always felt that was strength. We did many things together.

During Episodes

Many times, especially in the beginning, we were directed to marriage counseling. These sessions often would turn into fits of rage and I would walk away disgusted. They never seemed to help, but being unsure of what to do, I had to try. After many years of friendship and marriage I though that I knew her. In some sessions, though, she would verbally and brutally insult me. At first I was taken aback. After a barrage of insults, though, I resorted to defending myself. This was not the right thing to do, but the best defense is a good offense.

One counselor even suggested that she stay in the local hospital for three days just to get a handle on things. She refused, but I gladly accepted. They did not accept me. Many sessions would go by without any progress and the counselors would discuss anger management techniques with us. I would often retort to them that I don't want to manage the anger. I want to get rid of it. They generally had no idea how to take my frustration and after a while, I gave up.

The funniest rampage that comes to mind occurred during one of our later sessions with a counselor. After Terry became fed up with the session, she demanded to see another doctor. I did not have a problem with that. She did, however, request specific doctors. Now I don't claim to be an expert, but I would venture to guess that gynecologists are usually not associated with psychiatry.

I humored her and took her to his office. He seemed completely puzzled by my request to examine her. I explained the situation and her request, and he played along. He gave her a mock exam, offered her a candy and declared her fit. She was pleased to hear this and immediately exclaimed to me, "See, I told you I was okay." This made her feel better and calmed her down. I have to give the doctor a lot of credit, though. He never billed us for the visit, and joked with me about it for years to come.

After Episodes

The last aspect of counseling that I want to address is when she was released from the hospital. Every time they sent her home, she had to see counselors for a period of time. Inevitably, she would insist that I go, since it was entirely my fault. I went, figuring it was better to hear her scream for 30 minutes in a doctor's office than for three days at home.

I would tell the doctors what I knew and they would determine the best course of action. She would usually grow tired of these sessions within a few months, and we would stop going.

I tried to seek help, but every time that I did she would find out about it and panic at the thought. I tried to explain to her that I was the one going, not her, but this did not help. Eventually I gave up attempting, and just dealt with things on my own.

The most annoying thing to me about the counseling was the belittling that I received from certain family members. They proclaimed our situation as a marriage failure. We were going to counseling, and they were not.

I may have struggled for many years, but I am still standing. I can honestly say that I did everything in my power to remain by her. If I fail, it is not for lack of effort. It is more for lack of hope. The relationship is subjected to all of the pains of past as well as present.

I may have my faults, but turning and running is not one of them. I have always tried to protect and help her. Even at a high personal cost to me. I have accepted this fate over the years and tried my best to make it work.

Since I'd seen certain family turn on her, I knew my duty was not to. It is not a pretty thing that I do. Sometimes the process of these things is down right ugly. But they must be done. I have come too far, through too many things for quitting any of this now. It would be a sad event for me to succumb to defeat. I do not know that word.

Others have told me to divorce. They say that I have paid my dues and that I deserve better. The funny thing about that is the love you feel for someone is stronger than opinions. Although I think at times I can do better, I think back to the good times and realize that I still loved her. It just became increasingly harder to justify things done to me.

I know that in going through all of these things I have shown her countless times how much I loved her. It is better than a card. It is the acts and thoughts of the process that give them meaning. We had our problems and I tried my best to work them out.

In order to walk away, I must be at peace with myself. This is a very difficult thing. I do what I can. We are not perfect, but human. Trial and error, success and failure define us and make us who and what we are.

I have seen very weak people. That is because they have never had to do these kinds of things. They would readily walk away from minor things compared to what I've seen. That is what I believe defines character. The trials and struggles of such things are what make you or break you.

As people read of these things and realize that others go through them, they find their own lives are not so bad. That gives my writings a kind of silver lining. Others who just shake their heads at me have approached and asked why. I write stories and just try to tell others what it is like. Sometimes that is much easier than others. Counseling has always given me an outlet. Terry believes it has never done us any good. I believe that it has. Counseling is just one piece of the puzzle. Time will tell.

Priests and Clergy

It may shock you to hear this part, but it is true. Several times I spoke with clergy and men of the cloth. They had met Terry in the institutions and talked to her. They had informed me, more than once, that if I wanted an annulment or divorce, no one would blame me. They were considering what I had been going through. This took me back. I politely told them no.

This is a very difficult thing to discuss with clergy. You beg and plead for hope and answers. Medical situations are more easily understood and grasped. Mental illness can sometimes wear you down. In struggling with things, I have realized that some things just happen. There is no rhyme or reason.

Picking up the Pieces

Before She Gets Home

These are the times that I clean the house as best as possible and await her arrival. Any last minute things that I can take care of, I do. Upon her arrival, I will have to monitor her reactions. Once she is home, there will be counseling sessions and other doctor appointments that take precedence.

Cleaning up after episodes is usually an experience. I throw out a lot, and generally remove as many traces of the experiences as possible. I should take pictures and have tried in the past, but when she sees a camera she freaks on me. She usually denies everything, so what is the point?

Right after she is released from the hospital, she comes home aggravated and annoyed. For a few days she acclimates herself to being home again. She wanders locally and is irritable. This usually occurs as the medication wears off and her annoyance at the situation takes over. She has a very low tolerance level. I let her re-adjust and just stay out of her way.

Mum Is the Word

After things quiet down, the normal routines start to kick in. If you have any sense about it, you don't mention the episodes or you will get an earful. It doesn't matter what transpired. Either way, I know that I will hear about it, time and time again. I believe that this is her way of venting. Sooner or later, it will all come out.

I don't blame her for her frustration. I do not, however, like to be the target of it. I did not cause these things to occur. I have had to deal with this, just like her. I say nothing and hope each time is the last. We shall see.

Usually, as time goes on, she opens up and asks me many questions. Some I can answer, some I cannot. I only tell her a minimal amount. Details are sometimes sketchy. Specifics can be painful, and some memories I have locked away, not to be opened, ever.

There are details I will carry to my grave, and that is a fact. I do not do this for myself, but to protect her. If she knew certain things, it would kill her. If someone else discloses these things, I cannot help that. It will not be me. We have many times averted tragedy; she doesn't need these and other pieces of information. I just want this to be over with.

Accepting All of the Blame

Once we start discussing the past and her hospitalization, she inevitably blames me. It usually starts out with, "Why did you let them take me away? Did they have a court order? Did they have a warrant?"

No matter what my response, she scoffs at me. The truth is a useless commodity. She does not want to believe that at anytime it was for her own good. A number of times it was self-provoked. These were my fault as well. I just tell her, "It was my entirely fault. Blame me if it makes you feel better." She does.

The quiet times are generally when she reflects. She will pull things out of the air and throw them at me. Sometimes we talk openly. She generally gets annoyed at me, though. When I answer something honestly, the tone of the discussion changes. She believes it is my duty to protect her. I do. But above all, I am her friend. Sometimes, the truth hurts.

She has always failed to realize that during the most stressful of situations, decisions have to be made. These are not easy for me. At times they are very painful, but necessary. I take nothing lightly and do my best to look out for all concerned. I can't say that I am right every time, but I try to do what is right. I am, above all, only human. If she blames me for these things, then so be it. But remember that I never pushed her family away. They ran. Only her grandparents offered assistance. I appreciated it, but couldn't subject them to it. It is not fair to them.

The worst aspects of it all are the intensity and duration of things. It is the equivalent of dealing with cancer. You have to wake up every morning and face it, whether you feel up to it or not. Add to that the time it takes to pass through an episode completely and you are drained by the end.

Her Employment

I have always encouraged her to seek part-time employment. This seems to help her. The daily interaction with other people is good for her. It gives her spending money. She is a very good worker. She is conscientious and rarely misses time. The exceptions are when these events occur.

Unfortunately, she has lost her last three jobs. The good news is that I think that she has found much better employment. She has not had a severe episode in a few years and has held this job and thrived. Helping others has helped her. She enjoys it. I hope she stays at this job. They treat her well.

It is funny, but I have read reports that say that bipolar individuals fair much better when they are employed and have schedules to adhere to. For whatever the reason it keeps their minds focused on other matters. I find that fascinating and truthful. She had more episodes when she was unemployed than when she was employed. I believe that to be true from my experience with the situation.

The Reasons for All of the Trouble

Through the years I have found many reasons for all of the trouble. All of us have problems of one sort or another. It is just a matter of coming to terms with our past and resolving internal conflicts. More often than not, we are not even sure of the many things that influence us in our everyday activities. It is best for all concerned, especially our family, when we do so as quickly as possible. Otherwise we hold others accountable for things they had no hand in.

Teenage Years

Some of the initial catalysts for all of the trouble were events that occurred when she was a teenager. I have since learned that this was not the only problem, just the most significant in her mind. The information that I have collected on any specific event is minimal. I have left the true, in-depth details alone, and let the psychiatrists deal with them. I do not pry where I may not be wanted.

Our discussions on this subject have been brief, and I have never pressed her for information. If and when she felt the need to talk about it, she could come to me. I would gladly discuss it, but at her pace, and when she is ready. If it is never discussed any further, then so be it. The psychiatrists have told me that she is just realizing how much this event has bothered her. She has to come to terms with it herself, before she will ever be fully cured or let anyone in. It many never happen. Who knows?

Childhood Issues, Sibling Rivalry

Another issue that has come to light is the sibling rivalry that she has always had. Being the oldest, she always felt that she has always had more expected of her. She never felt that she was treated the same as her brothers or sisters. This is probably true of every kid that ever existed. Inevitably, parents tend to treat all of their kids differently. If there is a scale with which can measure who is treated better, then I would like to see it.

Although I have seen things in her family, I have personally not taken sides. However, I have defended her in the past. I have gone up against her parents and her sister at the same time on issues. They do not scare me, and given the option I would readily protect my family at anyone else's expense. They know this and weigh their approach to me. I do not start wars, but will gladly end them. They keep this in mind.

Ongoing Parental Things

There are other issues that are ongoing with Terry and her family. Far too many scrapes and battles to mention here. These are normal to any family. He said-she said things, that in the end are meaningless, but grate at ones nerves. I have seen my share of family woes and have learned that they can be petty and trivial. The important thing to me has always been that blood is thicker than water and family always stands by family, no matter what. There is an exception to this. It is when certain members cross lines in the sand that never should be crossed. You tear cloth at that point. The matter is then resolved.

Parents are parents and their children are children. It does not matter if the kids are fifteen or fifty. They are still your kids. You still worry and care about them until the day you die. You lecture and advise. These things are timeless. You just have to come to terms with differences of opinions.

Stress

The last reason for her troubles is stress. She has never handled stress well. In jobs and at home, she has had trouble dealing with these things. She shows anger abruptly and she lashes out. I try to keep stress down in the house and generally avoid these things. Families inevitably have stressful things occur. That goes hand in hand with raising children.

For the most part, things are okay. I let her go and try to avoid stressful things as much as possible. I take long walks to avoid problems. I try to prevent myself from saying something that I know will come back to haunt me.

She has been diagnosed with a stress disorder and that has contributed greatly to her problems. It has caused me to have to keep stressful situations around the house at a minimum. That may sound easy, but consider raising a family and not allowing stress into the house.

Essentially that means you have to shield the person from events. You must take the hits. That was always much better than the consequences. A day of agony was far better then two months of literal hell. Which would you choose?

Short Year Marriage

Through the course of events it is factual to say that some years we have a short year marriage. It usually starts after she comes out of an episode and lasts until she goes into the next. All that I mean by that is when you have to deal with these things for weeks or months, it reduces any reasonable time that you spend together.

I would say that it has not been a bad marriage. I would say that it has to meet specific criteria to be a marriage. I would say it is more of a bad relationship. All relationships have there good and bad times. Some just swing to and fro more then others. I have always felt that the ordeals that we go through define us as people. How can you fault someone for an illness? You can only find fault when they refuse to treat or recognize the illness if they have the ability to see it.

You take your wedding vows. You tell the minister, for good or bad, in sickness and in health, till death do you part, etc . . . There are times that you wonder when the good will come as opposed to the bad. We deal with the crosses that we bear. Whether they have splinters or thorns, they must be carried.

Hospitalization

Years that she is hospitalized are rough ones. It generally means that her episodes were much worse and she cannot be cared for at home. These are the hardest. Usually this translates into many household problems and situations that I had to skip over to get her help. These times grate on a marriage.

Even though some of these times are beyond description, I would not trade them for the world. She knows that even though I have had a hand in all of these events. I have never and will never do anything to harm her. I always take her best interests at heart

I would never say that I do not resent these things. I just don't place blame. Who would I blame anyway? When she is in the hospital, I lie in bed at night and wonder to myself, what it was, if anything, that I did wrong. I wonder what I could have done to prevent the things from happening.

Six-Month Marriage

Since the cycle of problems was relatively routine in the beginning, I learned how long things would usually be normal. I tried to spend quality time as a family. This does not always work out with scheduling, but we made do.

I have noticed that she clings at times. I understand this and try to support her. She is just as unsure as I am. We just approach it from different directions. When you love someone, you accept these things. I have never tried to change her. I am sure that she would try to change me, if she could come up with a way to do it. I am stubborn, pig headed, and insensitive. When it is all said and done, though, I have been there for her.

I normally react to an ongoing situation. It does not mean that I do not prepare. It just means that I do not overreact. I wait for her to reach a certain state before I take action. With any luck, I can just monitor. If she does not need hospitalization, she comes out of things more quickly and she has less resentment towards me. This allows for a more fluid household and marital transition.

There are activities that we do as a family and they are

good for all of us. Some activities I like to do on my own, but I have accepted the fact that she wants to be together, so I wave that private time. When I have a day off and can sneak out, I do. It is important to have quite time to ponder and reflect.

Anniversaries

The last and saddest issue to discuss is the anniversary. Unfortunately, our wedding anniversary falls in the time frame of the episode schedule. Many a year has gone by and we've had to deal with the issue of missing the anniversary. The years where she is hospitalized are the worst. She resents the fact that we cannot celebrate the day at all.

To date, we have skipped celebrating years and she reminds me of this fact constantly. It would be nice to have quiet time, but that has not occurred as much as we would like. Many years have gone by. We have done our best to deal with it, though.

Money and Credit

When dealing with medical issues, sooner or later you must come to terms with the money issues. When it comes to mental illness, most insurance plans will pay up to a lifetime amount for hospitalization and therapy. Although this limit is high in appearance, it is not that much money when treating an individual.

In The Beginning

At the very beginning of the episodes, cost really did not matter. Most therapy sessions were readily covered by insurance. Any other costs that I incurred were relatively minor. Doctor's visits were infrequent, so that was also not an issue.

As time went on and episodes became much more severe, the costs skyrocketed. It would take thousands of dollars and many years to bring this situation under control, hopefully.

Cancel Credit Cards

When I determined trouble was on the horizon, I would always cancel the credit cards. As a general practice, I don't use them anyway. This would prevent credit problems from popping up in the future. I always had a spare card around in case of emergencies. Over the years I learned to prepare now, or pay later.

To be honest, she has always been very good about the use of credit cards. She has never spent foolishly with them. We believe in debt-free existence. This has also allowed me to recover financially at the close of episodes. Actually, she is generally very good with money; I just can't take that chance when she is going through rough times. As she comes out of it, I reinstate everything. The house returns to normal, relatively.

Leave Minimal Cash Around

This is a good practice no matter what. I generally leave enough cash around to run the house and nothing more. When there are occasions that I need cash for something, I will get it at that point. As long as I have enough money for a cup of coffee and bait for fishing, I am happy. This has lent itself well to my experiences in this area. I have found that during episodes she has taken money several times and lost it or given it away. I have kept this damage to a minimum so far.

I also have never had a MAC card. Not due to financial problems, but because the temptation for her to use it would be too great. Most people don't realize that when someone has mental problems, they can still be very bright. They are fully capable to perform various tasks, even though their behavior may not be not up to society's standards. Even during an episode, I would never underestimate her. That is why I take the precautions.

No Insurance Blues

One year that Terry was hospitalized, I had no insurance. I was laid off at the time. The issues that presented themselves were more far reaching than you may think. One problem that I encountered was the initial hospitalization. When taken involuntarily, you are transported to a local hospital for psychiatric evaluation. They must make a decision within 72 hours whether to keep you and remand you to a psychiatric hospital, or release you.

The costs for these processes mount up quickly. You must consider doctors, ambulatory transportation, medications, and any other incidental costs. This does not include the hospitalization itself.

The good news is, if you have no money and you are on welfare or social security, your cost will be minimal. The courts cannot take what you do not have. You will pay something, but charity care will prevail.

The bad news is if you have any money, own a house, or are not a ward of the state, you will pay dearly. If not at the time of release, you will pay. At the close of one episode, I had a lean put on my house by the courts. I could not take all of the cash that I had and pay all of the bills with it. I was unemployed. That is a risk that I would not take. You may not think about these things, but some of us have to deal with them. Through no fault of my own, I incurred large medical bills.

It took me two years to pay off this debt. Again I became debt free. Some years, this is easier than others. I will somehow, someway, always own the shirt on my back. It may be ragged and worn, but will be mine.

The years when she can work, she does. She has her

own savings account and we use that to help pay medical bills. If we don't incur any medical debt that year, it is hers to spend. I give her a lot of credit, though. She is frugal with the money.

Don't Ask Family for Money

The issues of family and money have always fascinated me. They will get into your business until money is involved. In times of crisis, like these, they scatter.

Through all of this, I have never received one cent from her family. One set of grandparents is the only family of hers who even offered to help. I, in good conscience, cannot take money from them. It is not that they don't have money; it is the principle of the thing to me.

It would have been nice for her immediate family to offer it, though. I would not have taken it, but it would have been a supportive gesture on their part. I would never ask for money. I believe in pride and self-reliance. It has gotten me into trouble many a time. I still feel, though, that personal responsibility is vital.

Paranoia and Dementia

The first and foremost symptom she would display was paranoia. The definition of paranoia is, among other things, distrust. She would distrust anyone and everyone, including myself. There were times that she would suspect telephones, computers, and cable lines.

Our neighbor's antenna for ham radio reception always sparked a fire in her. It was located in a tree in the rear of his yard. For some reason, though, she would always insist on its removal. He accommodated graciously and removed it or relocated it to her liking.

The other thing that she would do during severe episodes was remove all of our phones. This would create a safety issue for me. I always had a spare hidden. The curious thing about it was she would also remove the answering machine as well. I tried to explain to her that this was just a recording device. She would not accept that so I unplugged it and she felt better.

The last thing that she always insisted on was the computer. I would have to unplug the modem and show her it was a stand-alone computer. She would accept this and go on her way. I would just plug it back in when I needed it and make sure she was not around. I was lucky that she was not computer savvy.

If for any reason there was a phone call before she removed the phones, she insisted on answering it. I pitied the person calling and hoped they had a hearing problem. No matter who it was, or what they were calling about, they received an earful. I am sure we were put on the do not call list for that.

Cell phones were another issue. To be caught on a cell phone was a critical mistake. I would hide mine and remove the battery. I hoped that she did not find it. I could not afford to let her hear it ring. She never did to my knowledge.

Neighbors would start coming to me during episodes and telling me stories. Many of them had to throw her out of their houses when she would not leave. She would show up at various times of the day and night and just talk. She would make no sense and just ramble on about the most bizarre things. Stories are still getting back to me about numerous events. I cannot confirm any truth to them.

Shell Game

The relocation of objects was one of her trademarks. She would take various objects and relocate and rearrange them to her own liking. Most of the time, this was a harmless practice. It involved her using nervous energy. She was keeping herself occupied.

I did not discourage this activity and honestly marveled at it. Sometimes I would just sit and watch. It was much more entertaining then you might think. As long as you did not question why she was doing something, you were okay.

She became a master at placing objects in the yard. She would take various things out of the house and arrange them in the back yard to her own liking. I didn't mind her doing it to anything that could be left outside, but discouraged her from doing it to electrical or other such weather-intolerant items. Generally she would not argue the point and just go get something else.

As long as I compromised, she was agreeable. This became my warped version of television. It is much more amusing than you could imagine. It's hard to describe. How often can you give details of a grown woman placing the most abstract of things throughout your yard with a vehement tenacity?

I just watched and listened. She actually had a method to it all as well. Isn't the human mind an amazing tool!

Phone Bills and Cries for Help

Calls to Family

During moderate and severe episodes she starts calling any and all relatives. Many of these people have not heard from her in years. At first she is pleasant and agreeable. It is more of a social thing. I have heard her be very nice. Then, as the conversation goes on, she runs out of courteous things to say and it gets ugly.

She starts insulting and picking on whom or whatever is bothering her. She can get vicious. I have heard her really insult me and other family members. I accept this and let her go. I take no offense because if she really meant it, we would not be together. These calls do not last minutes, but hours. These calls are to places all over the country.

Usually our phone bill skyrockets for the month that she does it. I pay the bill and hope it made her feel better. It did not do anything for me. I especially enjoy the questions that I get back. "Is there something wrong?" or "Is she all right?"

The funny thing to me is she will call back the same relative several times and virtually discuss the same things. I guess people are lonely, or maybe they just want to talk as well. She continues until she exhausts her list from her phone book. Round 2 then begins.

CALLS TO FRIENDS

The next round involves her friends. Many of these people she has not spoken to in years as well. The routine and comments are repeated. I, as well as others, am slandered. Again, I let her go, and I get the same questions back. Her friends call me back and ask, "How has she been?" "Is she okay?" etc . . .

What is funny to me is out of all of these people, only one has come by to help. She stayed 4 hours, couldn't take it, and left. "Thanks for the visit," I said. I deal with this 24 hours a day, 7 days a week. I know you are jealous, but I don't want to share. What can I say?

Everyone Else

The last list that she goes to is the neighbors and others list. She can start with contractors, neighbors, and whoever else she has a phone number for. She starts dialing and people come running to ask me what is going on. Once she completes this list, she has effectively alienated herself and the wandering begins. She starts looking for anyone that will listen.

If I am lucky, this entire experience will only run my phone bill up for 1 month. Usually after that, she removes the phones and the paranoia sets in. If this does nothing else, it cuts down my phone bill. I guess that is a warped way of looking at things.

Cost of Phone Use

When she comes out of an episode, she remembers making phone calls. However, she doesn't remember the quantity. She will ask me why the phone bill is so high. When she starts looking through the locations and phone numbers, she realizes it is all her family and friends. Trust me; she knows I'm not the one making these calls.

It hits her like a bolt of lightening. Even though she can't remember, she knows it was her. I usually get a puzzled look for a week or two. Then, after confirming the bill with a few of her friends, she knows it was true.

Paperwork and Filing

As I mentioned, one of the major problems that I have run into in the past is paperwork. It has taken me, at times, 3 months to recover documents and other paperwork that she has taken and strewn about the area. To this day, I am still finding paperwork that is 15 years old or older in the oddest of places. I find stashed bags, boxes and other containers full.

Every time I clean around the house, I find another container or bag of old paperwork. My current record dates back to 1981. It is a running joke between me and my oldest. It is bad when your kids pick on you over it.

I am still missing a number of items that I have seen her with, but could not recover. The scariest things that I have seen her take were social security cards, birth certificates, and paperwork to cars, trucks, and boats. By some miracle, I have always received them back. I usually keep all these materials locked up, but she sometimes finds ways to get at them.

I also try to hide all paperwork from doctors and hospitals. When she finds them, she gets angry at me and usually lectures me incessantly about letting them take her away. To date, I have kept things under control and she has only found minimal amounts.

Roll of Laminate

The funniest thing that she has done with paperwork involves her taping spree. During one stretch she found a few rolls of clear packing tape. She decided it would be a good idea to tape up numerous documents, papers, cards, licenses, and many other materials. To this day I find pictures and papers taped up. I believe she has found a new way to laminate.

On one occasion I had to present a taped-up card for processing. The clerk just looked at the card, then looked at me, and didn't say a word. Imagine a card with about 10 wraps of clear tape on it. It was a heavy little card. Once replaced, I destroy all that I can find. I still find one here and there. They do make me laugh, though. If find another taped-up credit card, I'm dying to use it just to see the expression on the cashier's face.

File Cabinets Are the Answer

A few years ago I purchased filing cabinets. I figured that instead of her usual unorthodox methods, I could keep up with her and file the materials in a logical manner. I could not have been more wrong.

I placed the cabinets in an accessible place and instructed her to put whatever paperwork was important in them. For a while, it was fairly reasonable. Then I noticed paperwork piling all over the cabinets. There were boxes and bags piled high on top of them. There were bags littering the floor all around the cabinets. I even found piles behind the cabinets. But, curiously enough, not one piece of paper was added inside the cabinets.

There is only one exception that she files religiously. She is adamant about filing menus to local restaurants. This is unbelievable to me but very funny. If you take a menu out and don't replace it, she knows. However, if you remove a medical or tax folder, she has no clue. This is one of the fascinating things that I have noticed through the years. Priorities are a beautiful thing.

At this point I had given up on her organizational skills in this area and just resumed shredding and filing myself. I laughed every time I found another bag of her filed paperwork and just shredded or filed the contents. I actually wore out shredders. I got maybe two years out of a shredder if I was lucky.

Every Saturday was my paperwork and trash day. I would go through the house and collect the paperwork that had accumulated during the week. You may not think that it is a lot. You would be mistaken. Some weeks it was light. More often then not, I found myself shredding Saturday night. If it was a rainy Saturday, I looked more intensely. There are always bags that are missed. I just tried to stem the flood.

Lock Up Important Documents

It is essential that anyone with these problems lock any important paperwork up and hide the key. If you value it, hide it. That is my rule of thumb. In the middle of an episode, anything and everything is fair game. You would be amazed at what can be gotten into. Any and all valuable paperwork must be out of sight and mind before the episode begins. If not, they will remember and look for it.

If you lock it away and keep it there, you will most assuredly find it after the episode has past. If on the other hand you do not, you may spend the next 2 months at your neighbor's house looking for it. I have recovered some paperwork 3 months after the conclusion of episodes. Believe me when I say, lock it up. You will save yourself enormous aggravation in the long run.

Shred or Hide the Rest

There is one alternative to locking up paperwork. Shred any paperwork that is not inherently valuable enough to lock up. This will also reduce the clutter in the house and allow you to clean up faster. If you do not want your materials to be spread around the neighborhood, lock or shred. Either way is very effective. You make the choice.

If you are unsure what to do with any paperwork, then my advice is to box it, label it, and take it to a family member's house to store it temporarily. You can easily recover it when the dust settles. Just make sure that it is a trustworthy family member. You never know.

What's Love Have to Do With It?

Running a House

When all is said and done, it is only practical to realize that the household still has to be maintained. You must remember that through all of this, the daily activities must be taken care of. This includes wash, dishes, food shopping, cooking, cleaning, etc . . .

I would never say that they continue uninterrupted. The fact of the matter is that things are dealt with as efficiently and effectively as I can muster, given the circumstances. The kids help but I above all try to let them be kids. It is, after all, better for them to be kids than tied up in this mess.

Over the years, I would not say that I am an expert in this arena; I just do what I can. There are aspects of this work that I like, and ones that I do not. We make do. I am generally a self-reliant individual anyway, so I can hold my own.

I have personally noted that I am not used to others doing things for me. I feel very uncomfortable when they do. I appreciate it. I just am not used to it, especially cooking.

When she comes out of these events, it is nice to relinquish some of the activities to her, but I find year round I still aid as time permits. My chores switch back and forth between household and property maintenance as events unfold.

Damage Control

The aspects of damage control elude many people, but they are a necessity. I do things at the onset in preparation of problems. This limits or eliminates trouble that may occur. As things wind down, I can return things back to normal and get the household functioning back on track. These activities include credit, cash, paperwork and vehicles, as well as others. It is the equivalent of dropping a monkey off of your back.

Once all of the components are back in place, I can relax for a few days and catch my breath. Some years I have a whopping six months before I have to pull up my boot straps and repeat the process all over again. This is how it is. It may not be pretty, it may not be practical, but it is the existence that some must endure.

There are good years that actually allow me to skip over sections of this and reduce my aggravation. I do not know ahead of time what will occur, though, so I have to be ready to repeat everything, every year.

After years of this you become much more competent at logistics. You only have certain times to get things done. You get proficient by necessity. Numerous chores must be completed in relatively short times. You learn fast how to choose what takes priority.

You even learn how and where to stow things away for future use. You would be surprised at where I have hidden things over the years. I have always found that most people cannot see the forest through the trees. When I know she will root through things, I place things right out in the open. Of course, I always put a spin on that.

This also lends itself well to Christmas presents. The kids look around, but do not find the gifts that I hide. One year I hid them in their room. They were 10 feet from the kids at all times. They never found them. They were in the ceiling right above their heads! Nothing heavy, I assure you.

When Family and Friends Step In

During a few episodes a family member thought they would help. Instead of talking to me or actually seeing her condition, they would start making calls to different agencies.

I remember dealing with various people that I did not even know.

Thanks, But No Thanks

One episode when Terry was relatively calm, a knock came on the door. It was a social worker called by a family member. The social worker came in. She looked over the house. She talked to me and the kids. Then, she talked to Terry. Although this irritated Terry, she was under control. The social worker left after not finding anything major wrong.

This incident set Terry off for over a week. After we were interviewed the worker left and I bore the brunt of her wrath for many days. Once I calmed her down again, she was okay for the rest of the episode. I had another counselor come towards the end of the episode to check her out. As long as she knew what was going on, and who was coming, she was all right. If, however, you didn't inform her, you were taking a big chance that it would backfire.

Hell Hath No Fury

The worst family intervention occurred when a family member called crisis intervention without telling me. A knock came at my door. Four state police officers and a counselor came in. They were told that Terry was a threat to herself and my kids. A half an hour later they took Terry out in handcuffs.

She resented this with a passion and fought them well. She was taken to a local hospital for evaluation. After keeping her overnight for observation, they released her the next day. Now she was free and mad. Do you want to venture to guess as to whom she took this out on? To this day, I still hear about it. The relative, though, is nowhere to be found. By the way, she does not know who it was and I will not tell her.

Infrequent Visits

Through the many years of dealing with these things, you could count the number of visits that her family made on one hand. At the first sign of trouble they would break off all contact. I would hear from them after the episodes finished. They would ask how she was. Thanks for your concern, I would say sarcastically.

All of the time she was in the hospital she was visited once by immediate family. Not to be picky, but if I could handle work and the kids and running the house without their help, and still manage to see her almost every day, where were they? This nonexistent support has lasted up until the present. At this point, I just keep my mouth shut for her benefit. If they were my family, I would disown every last one of them. But I leave that up to her. I say nothing.

When she was home, I would get a visitor sporadically. They would come, see her for maybe an hour and leave. I would get a call later asking how I put up with such things. I would retort, "What choice do I have?"

One family friend called and said she would watch Terry for a couple of hours so I could get some food shopping done. After she arrived, I gave her a few pieces of advice and some phone numbers. I had the oldest help and keep an eye on things. I took the youngest with me. I went to the store for 2 hours and came back. My friend was frazzled. She jumped in her car upon my return and left without saying a word. When they called a week later she informed me that she had enough. She was sorry, but could not handle it. I told her not to be sorry.

Unfortunately, I have had to handle this for many years, so for me, it was just another day in the park. I understand some people have trouble with these things. I did, too, at the start. The learning curve that I had to overcome was brutal.

Baptism by fire, though, has its advantages. It toughens you up and strengthens you to deal with things.

The benefit from this is that it has made me better at my job. When I have to deal with things at work, I just shrug my shoulders and deal with things. I have learned that things happen. You don't fuss and complain, just deal with them. This gets things done much quicker. I don't create trouble. I alleviate it.

The Older the Better

It may be interesting to note that through all of this, the older generation has been the most supportive. They have offered me assistance and whatever aid they can muster. They have also visited the most and at times, inspired me. It is nice to hear good things in the middle of such events. Terry's grandfather has told me that he admires me. He respects the fact that I have stood by her and endured numerous things. He is the one and only family member that I truly respect. These words coming from him mean a lot to me.

The thing that truly amazes me is her grandparents always have a kind word to say. At the depth of the valley of these events, a soft, gentle word can make all of the difference. They offer wisdom and guidance, which is usually in short supply. Just a pat on the back or a shake of the hand with a brief show of support usually helps get me through to the next crisis. I will forever be in their debt.

Friends

Nov 4

The power of souls is not measured still. It resides in the heart out of sight. Yet for all of its mystery and unknown force, it gives us all such delight.

Man shall never understand God's strength of soul, given at birth to us all. For friendship is power and no matter the evil, in its hands it will surely fall.

A care and a love will always prevail. For kindness will heal any wound. The given ability carries us forth, until one day it resides in a tomb.

When God calls it back to be refreshed and reborn, he always shall find its place. It walks on this earth in one form of life, and lives somewhere else in space.

You are my friends and will always be so. My words will always fall short. The feelings I get carry me along, as you are my home and my port.

I hope and I pray to always be worth, your time and your love so supreme. For the value of all of your love has warmth, and has always been somewhat a dream.

To awake one day and realize its loss would be such a strike at the heart. The total effect shall never be known, as I would hope that I would soon restart.

Working and Jobs

Most people deal with social security when they turn 65 or older. In this area, though, mental illness can be considered a disability and you can be eligible for social security at a much younger age.

The reasons vary with the individual. It all comes down to the degree of disability and the prognosis. A competent doctor can provide the necessary information. If, however, there is hospitalization involved, the likelihood goes dramatically up.

A Decision

A number of years ago, I made the decision not to apply for social security for her. We led a relatively normal life, considering the events. I believed that she would be able to work and earn an income on her own. In the last few years she has earned a decent income. She has progressed and is doing much better. The signs and symptoms have changed some. I believe, though, that with proper therapy and counseling, she will be all right. Getting her to therapy, well, that is another issue.

I do not personally believe that social security is the appropriate answer in most cases. Family and church support is a much better option. Besides pooling all of the resources of the local community, it gives people a good feeling to help others in need. Isn't that what it is all about?

Self-Reliance

If it is at all possible, let the person work and earn an income. The extra money earned never hurts. It also gives them the satisfaction of earning for themselves and self-reliance for their actions. The ability to get out and interact with others is also an added benefit. Any and all social interaction is crucial for recovery. The value of self-worth will also be restored quicker.

It does not matter the job or duties that need to be performed. Generally speaking, they will do an excellent job. They don't usually have the inhibitions that the rest of us are subjected to. The other thing to consider is that I have personally seen individuals who were absolutely brilliant in their areas. You would never even think they were capable of things. It is just something to keep under consideration.

Recent studies on the matter have concluded that someone who suffers from Bi-Polar is much better off having a routine schedule. A work and home regiment are therapeutic in actuality. I have found this to be the case in my experiences as well. When Terry was not employed, things were much worse.

The Stories

"I have seen the darkness and the light, both have their own affect.
I have known the cold and felt the frost and been subject to neglect.
If choice be given the day would go to the essence of the glow.
The brightness deep inside the case of soulful ones won't show."

City Life

Many times through the years Terry wandered away and I did not hear from her for long stretches of time. Most of these incidents occurred without raising much of an alarm. There were, however, times that created a panic in me. I worry about her all of the time when I don't know where she is. This is a natural reaction. This incident struck a nerve with me because of the degree of danger. It is funny to say, though, how people generally don't bother with someone who is mental. The degree of uncertainty and the behavior leave too much to chance. This gives a false sense of security. You never really know what people are capable of.

The Silence before the Storm

It all started out as a relatively normal day. She was in a calm mood and there were no signs of trouble. I was working around the house and she was in the yard. I could hear her talking and since she was calm, I paid her no mind. After a while there was silence.

I went outside to see if she was okay. I looked all over the property and in the woods by the house. I did not find her. I walked the neighborhood. No one had seen her for a while. Now I started to become worried. I went back to my car and drove the area. I cruised the town and the local places that she visited on her travels. I found no trace of her.

I called the state police and informed them to keep an eye out for her. They knew her and gladly obliged. They said they would contact other local agencies as well. At least that made me feel better. I still had no idea where she was.

I continued to search for her myself with the youngest in tow. I left the oldest home with a neighbor and a phone just in case she called or a report may came in from the police. After about 2 hours we did receive a call. She called to tell us that she was at a bus station. She was confused but at least gave me a little information.

She informed me that she was in the city. This is about 20 miles from my house. I wondered how she got there. She said she wanted a ride and said a friend of hers drove her there. I asked her who it was. She couldn't remember. She then informed me of her location at the transit bus terminal. I told her to stay put and that I would be right there.

Mean City Streets

I immediately called the local police and alerted them as to the situation. The detective that I spoke to was very nice and gave me instructions and phone numbers for assistance. He said he would dispatch a car over to that location and check it out while I was on my way down to get her. I gave him her description and he graciously accommodated.

Upon arriving at the bus terminal I saw the police car. I spoke to the officers and they informed me that no one matching that description had been there. I decided to call back home and check in. My oldest informed me that he had received a call from a local hotel. A supervisor had called our house on her behalf to inform us that Terry was at a parking garage. Now it was beginning to make sense.

I called the hotel and informed them that I would shortly be there. I drove over to the garage and spoke to the supervisor. They informed me that Terry had just left. They tried stopping her but she wouldn't listen.

I started to comb the immediate area and look for her. I couldn't find her. I became extremely worried and decided to call the local police and alert them of the news that I had. They informed me that they would keep an eye out for her. They asked me if I had a photo of her.

I dropped the photo off at the police station that they asked me to. I spoke to the sergeant at the desk and gave him all of the information that I had. He asked me to call back in the morning if I had heard nothing. I decided to look through the area one more time before I headed back to my house. I did not find her. It had now been 12 hours since I had seen her last.

I arrived back home and decided to wait things out for awhile. I made dinner and waited for a call, any call. I didn't sleep much that night. It was an eerie calm. I worried all night. When morning came, I decided to begin my search again. I had heard nothing for many hours. There was no news from any of the police agencies. I was asked to come in and fill out a preliminary missing persons report.

As I entered the police station for the second time I wondered if I would ever see her again. I knew that in her state she was vulnerable. Many thoughts went through my mind and I was desperate to find her. I filled out all of the paperwork required. I spoke to a detective. He said to call him if anything else developed or if I heard from her. He informed me not to worry and that they would do everything humanly possible. It was too late. I was beyond worried. I took his business card and decided to look over the city on my way back home. I drove the streets to no avail.

When I arrived home I called anyone that I could think of that might have seen her in that area. No one had seen a trace of her. I did some house work and cleaning to keep my mind off things. It distracted me long enough to become relatively calm again.

Return of Prodigal Daughter

I was home about 2 hours when I heard her in the yard. Apparently, she had received a ride back home. An unknown police officer gave her a ride out of the city to township limits. After that, the details that she gave became sketchy.

Now she was quite angered with me. She wanted to know why I had not gone to the bus terminal to pick her up! I tried to explain my ordeal to her but she did not want to listen.

I called the detective and informed him of her arrival. He said he was glad that it worked out and if I had any more problems, to call him. I thanked him and hoped that I would not need his services again.

Terry was in an agitated state now. She demanded to know why I had left her there in the city. Why had I not come when she called? Did I not care enough about her? I heard these things for hours. I had not slept any real amount in a few days. I was tired. Being thankful that she returned safely, I just wanted a nap.

I made the calls to the agencies that were looking for

her to let them know that she was okay. I thanked them and hoped to get a couple of hours of sleep. Terry had other plans. She verbally tested my hearing capabilities and limits. I was happy when she finally ran out of steam and decided to take a nap herself. This gave me a chance to nap.

I slept a few hours and awoke to find her gone again. This time, though, she was in a neighbor's yard. I decided to wait her out and do yard work myself. She came back home after a while and acted as if nothing had happened. I was glad. I didn't feel like suffering anymore that day, anyway.

So ended her little adventure. I never found out who ferried her either way. The details that I have pieced together since then are limited. I know where she was and who gave her partial rides. I know that she walked a number of miles on her own. I just want to thank all of those involved for their help. It is one of those many events that I am just glad that everything turned out all right. God watches over drunks, little children, and her.

Book Fair

Everyday something different would happen. For a while, it kept me on my toes. Usually I could just let things run their course. They would go away in their own sweet time with little or no interference from me. Occasionally, they created problems that I had to deal with right away.

Reading is Fundamental

A few times a year, our local school holds a book fair. This is when they exhibit many books and sell them at our library. Usually I go down and purchase a book or two for my own pleasurable reading. This incident created a whole new set of circumstances for me.

From the best that I can piece together, it went like this.

Terry and my youngest went down to the local book fair. She was in a relatively good mood when she left. I thought there was going to be no problem. I was in for a surprise.

A few hours after they left, my son returned home with a friend and his mom. Terry was not with them. They were not sure where she was. I didn't worry about her. I figured that she was still at the school or library.

My son walked in the house with a couple of books. This was pretty much the normal thing upon his return. I figured that Terry had had money when she left, so it didn't worry me. He didn't tell me anything was wrong. He went up to his room and everything seemed fine.

Terry returned later that day a little out of sorts, but not all that bad. I went about my business and didn't pay any attention. The next day, though, the reality set in. I received a call from the school about her antics at the fair. She was in rare form I was told.

The woman on the phone was happy that we helped in the cause. She said she was grateful that we were willing to make such a large purchase on the school's behalf. I knew I was going to regret this. I had to ask what the heck she was talking about.

Apparently Terry decided to buy a large number of books. You may ask why. I don't have an answer. All I know is that she filled out the form and the books would be there in a day. They were already ordered.

The books arrived the next day and we paid for them. However, most of them disappeared shortly afterwards. Some she gave out, some she lost. The rest are around the house somewhere. It was the only time that I allowed this to happen. After that, we would not allow the school to charge us for these kinds of acts.

Considering it was for a good cause, I let it go. To be taken advantage of sometimes happens. You just try to keep it to a minimum. There are times when this is easier than it sounds.

Overall, though, we have fared well considering what could have happened.

Events have occurred at school a few times. We have always dealt with them as efficiently and as effectively as possible.

To the school's credit, they have not overreacted. The other state agencies that have also been involved to date have all performed on a professional level. I can't recall one instance where problems were blown out of proportion or exaggerated due to improper handling of events.

Can't Find Any Paper

We all write on whatever is handy when we need to record things. I have jotted things down on envelopes, pads, and pieces of cardboard and then transferred the note or measurements to more appropriate stationary. We do this constantly in our everyday lives.

As the years went by, I noticed that Terry would write things on whatever materials she could get a hold of, some even more unorthodox then others.

Writing on the Car

When strange things happen, we are not always aware that they are going on. Since they are not expected, we don't look out for them. This incident actually happened to me. Hopefully, it doesn't happen again.

One day while I was going out to lunch with a coworker, I was shocked to learn something. As I approached my car the individual informed me that there was something on it. Upon closer inspection I found the markings to be writing. They were hard to decipher, but sporadic words could be made out. They were etched into the paint on my car with some sort of pen, I presumed.

I told the other fellow that my kids must have done it and played the whole thing off. When I arrived at home after work that day, I took a closer look. Terry must have written the message days before because the lettering was slightly weathered. Most of it was legible, but worn enough that it was not noticeable.

I began to wonder how long it had been on my car. Thinking back, I did not recall a day when Terry seemed upset with me or severely out of character. The writing, though, pointed to her in its language and structure.

I compounded off the remnants of the writing and buffed and waxed the spot. The bulk of the letters were gone, but I could still see traces. As it was an older car, it didn't bother me that much. I went inside the house to inquire about it. Terry said that she wrote on the car because she was mad at me.

Now I was puzzled. I asked her why she was mad at me. She couldn't remember but said she had a good reason. I had heard this many times before and knew not to press her. For the most part she was behaving and for whatever reason, she decided to forego paper and write on my car.

Since no permanent damage was done, I decided not to worry about it. A few years later when I sold the car, the writing was still there if you looked closely. The new owner never noticed it and the car has been out of my possession for 10 years now. Maybe, somewhere out there, the car is still being driven and the writing is still there.

After reading this, everyone should check their cars.

The vehicle may still be driving around with a message of madness etched into it. You never know.

You can tell that through all of the years and all of the events I have developed a warped sense of reasoning with myself. I have always wondered about her rational for writing on my car. If I was going to write on a car, I would write on the driver's side, not the passenger's. This has always bothered me about this act. It was like she didn't want me to find the writing, but someone else. She didn't have an answer for this, but maybe that was her intent!?

Clothes Tree

Planting the Seed

A few years ago the seed to the clothes tree was planted. This was no ordinary tree. During one the episodes, Terry spent a lot of time outside. While outside she favored, for one reason or another, a tree in our back yard.

Around this tree she placed many objects. They were diverse. She laid storm windows, figurines, plates, and many other objects against or in that tree. The most predominant feature was the clothes that she placed in it. This tree had virtually all of her clothes spread out throughout its branches. This in itself was no small feat. When I say this tree was full of clothes, I mean full.

It was actually an impressive thing to see. I asked her why she placed all of the clothes there. She responded that she wanted to share them with the neighbors. That made sense? I watched her continuing to place objects around the tree. She even went so far as to rest a spare tire along its roots. Don't ask.

PRUNING

After the seed was planted, I watched her prune the tree for days. She would take a piece of clothing here, or an object there. The contents of the tree dwindled a little, but not a lot considering the amount of material around it.

When I heard her offer our neighbors clothing from the tree, I nearly burst at the seams. They gave me a puzzled look and just said no thank you. I wondered what went through their minds, but I didn't have time to ask.

As the weeks past, she picked at the tree less and less. Other things kept her occupied. I figured it was time to harvest the tree. I wanted to get everything that I could back inside.

HARVESTING

This was the time of year for harvesting. Some people picked apples and some peaches. I was favored with picking a clothes tree. I climbed the branches and started to throw down clothes. Once we emptied the contents of the tree, I cleaned around the base and roots. I did a number of loads of wash to clean what I could. Certain clothes were ruined and I just threw them out. The clean up took a couple of days and the tree was soon bare.

After this episode I have found numerous things buried in the ground around the tree. I still go out occasionally with the metal detector and find things there. She has buried kitchen utensils, trinkets, and many other small items there. I have found broken glass from many objects that I cannot identify now.

I have taken that tree down since then, but will always remember when it bore fruit of a most unusual nature. The vision of that tree with clothes hung throughout its branches will forever be etched in my mind. I still shake my head at the thought.

There are times when you can laugh. This is a valuable commodity when you are going through these things. I try to laugh at some of these events. They are quite funny. Unfortunately, they have never outnumbered the times that make you cry. That is the unfair balance that you must learn to deal with.

Tree

Jan 25

In life the moments shall pass us by and we never grip the sum.
The deeds and acts encompass those who drink their lives as rum.
But those of us who take all in and know what there shall be.
Will always look at every leaf as part of greater tree.

Most look upon the mighty oak and only see the shade.
They forget the fact that greatest plant relies on tiny blade.
Not grass I speak but flopping piece of green that hangs on branch.
It gives so much back to mother that she shall have a chance.

These words hold more then botanic thoughts consider point of fact.
They speak of contributions surely made and show us how to act.
For Mighty oak is not a tree but society in the world.
Think not yourself as a leaf, think more a tool unfurled.

Give back what you may find you can and offer your own gift.
Then all shall blossom and enhance the strength and not succumb to rift. A
leaf will grow and collect the sun and send its life juice back.
When death and fall shall grasp its stem and brown upon the lack.

In order for the world to move in direction best for all.
Send best that you may become until the day is fall.
Others may not follow path yet view your effort real.
It matters not what they may attempt as long as you appeal.

With violence and death so plain in everyday events.
Most important parts of motions come from little ones pretense.
Not significant part deemed by some but kindness breeds aware.
Some will turn and glance a bit while others stand and stare.

Most important point of all I write consider real and true.
Act like you are on a walk and perform the path as new.
I may not yield a greater lead or shape the effort so.
I only do what I see as best and stroll down path I know.

DIFFERENT IS INTERESTING

One of the many fascinating aspects of all of this is the everyday behavior and events. Even when she is very much "normal" she still has quirks, like all of us do. You just learn to look at things from her point of view, whatever that may be at times.

WIND CHIMES

She has always had a liking for wind chimes. This in itself has never been a problem. I like them myself. The fact is she does not hang them outside, but inside. This would not bother me except that she has always liked to hang them on doorknobs, cabinet handles and other such things. To open a medicine cabinet every morning and fight a wind chime to get out a razor can be such fun. I always remove them but they migrate back to the knob by the time I get home. I asked her, "Why put it there? Can't we hang it up out of the way?" "No." She responds. "I like the sound it makes when I open the door." You have no idea the things that I put up with to make her happy sometimes.

Bird Feeders

Almost any rural house in America has a bird feeder in the back yard. We have a number and it is a joy to sit and watch the birds feeding at them. I enjoy watching the different species of birds and their interactions. It amazes me how they all get along for the most part. Maybe people ought to spend more time watching birds and see how it is done. Nature can do it. It has made me realize that man isn't as smart as he thinks he is.

Anyway, Terry enjoys the feeders and adding food and looking for different birds all of the time. On a good day we will discuss how we watched a different woodpecker, hummingbird, or finch than we normally see. I have seen many more types then most would think out of my kitchen window.

There are species that she doesn't like. This is where it gets good. I will look out and see certain birds that drive her crazy. She will run out the back door screaming and shouting and chasing all of the birds away. I watch and just enjoy how the second she turns her back, they return. It is a cat and mouse game that she never wins.

Throw In Squirrels

Then the squirrels join in. They torment her constantly. I have seen them swinging on the feeders and marvel at their ability to hang on. I really like to watch them sit below a feeder and try to figure out how to get up on it. Sometimes they are very successful. Through the years I have learned how to hang feeders to discourage their efforts.

I shake my head at Terry, who will hang a feeder and then complain. I try to tell her that the squirrels will get to it. She won't listen and she gets mad at me for allowing them to eat all of the food. I figure if they can get to the food, they deserve it. They don't have wings. I just don't like certain greediness.

One day when I was coming home from work I heard a noise. I looked up above and saw a squirrel carrying one of our feeders. I couldn't believe how he didn't sit and feed. He tried to carry the entire feeder away. This was too much for me. I proceeded to chase him from our yard into our neighbor's yard. He ran across a number of tree limbs through our yard. He crossed the street over my head and proceeded to run on branches on my neighbors' tree. The squirrel did the best he could but I scared him into releasing the feeder.

Once the feeder fell, he began to chatter and let me know how annoyed he was at me. I told him to file a grievance with the complaint department—Terry! Funny, but I never received a written complaint.

Don't Dial 911 If You Are Nuts

There were many times that I had to deal with operators. Generally speaking, they were very understanding and helpful. At times, I did not envy them. To deal with frantic people all day is frustrating to say the least. A phone call from a mental person is not a joyous thing. If it does not fray your nerves, I would be surprised.

The worst thing about dialing an operator during an episode is being able to actually talk and get across my point. To try to have conversation while a screaming match is going on right behind you is most difficult. The information that is relayed is less then accurate. You must constantly correct any errors.

This incident actually occurred during one of her most severe episodes.

I was in the living room playing monopoly with the kids. Terry was in the kitchen. She was relatively quiet for a long time. I started to hear her shouting and speaking very loudly. I went into the kitchen to investigate. I found her over by the kitchen sink with a knife in her hands. It was a very large butcher's knife.

The sight of it and the way that she yielded it was not a pleasant thing to see. I asked her to put it down for fear that she would cut herself or me. She did not comply. She waved the knife around and made a threatening gesture with it. I again asked her to put it down. She told me to stay away and insisted she would use it. Now she had crossed into a different arena.

Up to that point, I would have let it go. But to threaten the kids, or myself, raised my level of concern. In becoming a threat to others, a much higher degree of alarm went off. Now I knew I had to step in and get her help. When she looked away from me for an instant, I disarmed her. I took away the knife.

She gave me a look and went to the phone. She dialed 911 and began telling the operator a barrage of stories. I just sat back and let her go. The direction and content of the stories changed constantly. Her tone finally came down and the conversation drifted to a more casual and relaxed state. The operator asked her if I could have the phone and she gave it to me. She walked away and went into the other room while we spoke.

As I gave the operator the information that she requested, she informed me the police were on their way. I informed her of the knife incident, but told her that she was much calmer now. I gave her all of the information that I could. She told me just to stay on the phone until the police arrived. I talked about various things and waited.

When the police arrived they knocked on the front

door. My oldest opened the door and let them in. Two officers came in and told me to hang up the phone. I said good-bye to the operator and complied. They asked me to go to the porch with them and I did. While on the porch they asked what had happened and I told them the whole story.

Terry was upstairs now and I told them that. They asked her state and what medications she was on. One officer went upstairs to talk to her. The other stayed with me. I guess it was considered a domestic dispute case at that point. I sat on the step and talked to the officer. Having been through these things before, I was used to it.

When the officer returned from talking to Terry he wanted to talk to me again. He said he wanted to take Terry into custody and have her evaluated. I laughed at him and said good luck. You better call for backup. He gave me a puzzled look and asked why. I told him it took 4 officers last time and they barely won even with my help. He called for backup.

Obviously, I thought to myself, this guy never had to deal with this kind of situation. To even consider just 2 people taking her into custody was ludicrous. On a good day maybe 3 people could do it. I would not even attempt without a fourth handy, though.

As the third patrol car pulled up, I ushered the kids to a neighbor's house. They didn't really need to see this. I tried at times to shield as best as I could. I can't say that I always succeeded. The police made a coordinated effort and took her into custody without too much effort. She had fought them, but no more than usual. It still took all 4 of them to control her!

They decided to take her to the local hospital for evaluation. I informed them that the hospital in question did not have a psychiatric unit. They were aware of it. Upon arrival, they left her handcuffed and turned her over to the care of the attending physician. This facility had handled her before. They questioned her, gave her a physical and determined that she was neither a threat to herself or others. Her behavior, although eccentric, was not against the law.

Free At Last

She was released shortly afterwards. She refused any rides and insisted on walking home. I reminded her that she was about 15 miles from home. She didn't care. It was now late at night. She would not take a ride from me. She left the hospital and started to walk home.

She walked about ½ mile when she came across a supermarket. There was a truck out front and they were delivering supplies. She walked up to the two gentlemen there and began talking. She was pleasant at first. Then she became very loud.

After a few minutes, she started screaming at them. They were taken aback. It was now about 2 AM and I'm sure they were not used to this. The shift manager came out to see what the trouble was. Upon seeing Terry, he called the police.

A patrol car showed up shortly afterwards and picked her up. The officer did not handcuff her. He put her in the back seat. He then drove her to the limits of the township and dropped her off. At this point she started walking. After a couple of miles a state police officer saw her on the shoulder of the road. He then picked her up and drove her home.

She appeared at my door tired and a little worn. She was generally in a decent mood. The police had told me that they had kept an eye on her on the trip home. They just wanted to make sure that she was okay. She came home and took a nap. She seemed okay after this incident. It was just one of those things.

The supermarket shift manager remembered her later that year when we were in his store. He had trouble placing her, though. She looked familiar. He just couldn't figure out why. I decided not to elaborate. We use that supermarket to this day. He still can't figure it out.

Don't Go Shopping

When things did not seem all that bad, I would go shopping. We always needed food or other things around the house. The quieter times are when I tried to catch up on chores. There were many times that Terry did not want to go. There were times that she did. It was a judgment call whether I would chance taking her or not. Most of the time she was a little enthusiastic but relatively behaved. Other times I had to drag her from a store and pray that the police did not pursue.

This story happened during one of her moderate episodes.

One day, when I had to go to a local department store, Terry accompanied me. She was in a calm mood. She was a little energetic, but manageable. We entered the store and I proceeded to pick up the things that we needed and place them in the shopping cart. Terry decided that she wanted to check out fabrics and materials. She headed that way. As I went through my list, I heard sporadic yelling. I knew that it was her. I figured that maybe she was just being loud. I did not hear any pages or see any management going to where she was. I stopped shopping, though, and decided to investigate.

As I entered the department that she was in, I noticed an older woman who seemed quite perturbed. I knew that I was closing in. Upon closer inspection I found various draperies and fabrics strewn about. The materials were laid out over a number of shelves and boxes. Terry was nowhere to be found, though. Other usually organized racks and bins had their wares emptied onto the floor. The trail was getting hotter. As I approached the blankets and bed linen area, I noticed sheets and pillowcases out of their packages and strewn about. This meant that I was closing in on her.

I found her down an aisle with lamps and mirrors. She was dismantling the lamps and rearranging the lampshades.

She seemed a little out of sorts, but generally speaking, calm and content. She was just very energetic. I knew that I had to shuttle her out of there before management had us thrown out. I convinced her to follow me to the front exit. The management team was starting to amass and I heard numerous complaints from the clerks. Time was running out.

As I led her through the front door, a police car showed up. I walked her past and opened the door to my car. She sat down and I walked around to the driver side. I looked back to see the manager giving his complaints to the officer. He was pointing in our direction and complaining rather loudly. I closed the door, started the car and proceeded to make a break for it. I rounded the corner and backed in behind a building to elude the police. I watched the patrol car pass and I shot out and went the other way.

When I arrived home, I shuttled Terry into the house and waited for the police to arrive. They never did. I went shopping again later that week. I did not take Terry, though.

Handcuffs and Gurneys

There are times in your life that you do not want to recall. They are painful and beyond speech. Unfortunately they are forever etched in your thoughts. Flashes appear to you without warning or notice. Images from the past grate at your soul and bring you to tears in an instant. Try as you may to subdue or forget you can't. The worst of it is that there are not one or two memories, but many. If you succeed in locking away one such thought, another appears. This is not a battle to be won. A draw would be much appreciated, though.

The worst of these events come right to the surface. They grip you in grief and don't let go until the memory has past. This sometimes takes a few seconds, but can last much longer. Once past, another appears. These events can overwhelm at times.

A Mattress Fortress

An incident that I will never forget started out with Terry in an agitated state. Her emotions were swinging drastically from pleasant to thoroughly depressed. I just tried to monitor things and did not get in her way.

As night fell she became deeply depressed. She grabbed my son, went upstairs and barricaded herself into a bedroom with a mattress. She would scream things out to me, and not talk sensibly. This went on far too long for me. I was concerned for the welfare of my son. She would not send him out. I tried to convince her to release him to no avail.

I grabbed the phone and called the police. Having spoken to them frequently, they knew us, and our situation. Two officers showed up shortly afterwards, and they spoke to me on my front porch. We discussed weapons in the house and anything else that may be construed as a threat. I knew of nothing at her bedroom location.

The senior officer decided that he would investigate and I showed him where she was. He proceeded cautiously and spoke a few words to Terry. Her screaming and tone made it clear that she had no intention to remove the barricade and come out. She would not release our son. The concern on the officer's faces was not reassuring to me. I knew that look all to well.

We met back downstairs for a conference and decided our course of action would be to rush her and get my son out of harm's way. At their command, we broke through the barricade and I grabbed my son and removed him to a neighbor's house.

Our next task was to take Terry into custody and handcuff her. This would require two more officers and a lot of luck. You must realize that mental patients are quite strong. No matter how strong the individual under normal circumstances, as the adrenaline flows, they get much stronger. They tend to thrash and fight like demons. It is no easy task to subdue them.

After a bitter struggle, we handcuffed her. We fought again to get her into the police car. Once in the car she kicked at the windows and doors and screamed. This went on for a few minutes while we decided where to take her. The hospital that was agreed upon was twenty minutes away. I would meet them there after locking things up.

The police car drove away and I looked at the face of my son. He had a scared and worried expression that melted away my normally solid exterior. Again, I was left to pick up the pieces and try to make sense of this.

What do you tell a child? This is not right or wrong, just real. After many years, words just don't describe it. I gave up rationalizing any of this. My oldest and I are probably scarred beyond repair now. There is not much more to say. My only hope is that the youngest doesn't have to go through this.

We were on our way to the hospital. Not a word was spoken the entire way. We arrived at the emergency room and rushed in. They were strapping Terry to a gurney and sedating her. She would be held there for no more then 72 hours and then, if determined, transferred to a psychiatric hospital. We had been down this road before.

After a few hours it was decided that a temporary psychiatric facility was in order. She was again transferred to another hospital, twenty-five minutes away. I drove there to help support her. After two days she was placed in a longer care psychiatric hospital.

Long Days and Lonely Nights

After work each day, I would get my son and drive to

the hospital. These were long hours of grief for me. I tried to make light of the situation, but children are not stupid. They know what is going on. I kept the stress down as best I could.

As I turned into the hospital parking lot I could see her standing by the window and waving to us. My son would wave back. She knew about what time we were coming and waited on our arrival. When we entered the hospital, Terry would light up.

When we entered the ward, she would show us off to the other patients. She was heavily medicated, but would tell us whether the food was good or bad. She would inform us of staff members and breakthroughs in sessions. She was generally pleased with her treatment by the staff, and so was I.

After a month we appeared in court at the facility. A judge spoke to me in chamber and the doctors and I decided that all treatments were working and she could be released soon. After a few days, she was released. This was the first bit of good news that I received for awhile.

Initially she was fine when she came home. After a few days, the medication wore off and she became very irritated with me. She slowly improved, though, and was relatively normal in a few weeks.

She remembered very little of the whole event. She just asked why I had let the police take her away. I tried to explain, but she became angered at me. She asked if they had a search warrant. She wanted to know where the court order was. I gave up and told her it was my fault. She accepted this. It is always easier for her to believe whatever transpires is my fault. Peace again reigned in the house, for a while.

A month later she would bring up the fact that the entire event should not have happened. She did nothing wrong and should not have ended up in a mental institution. This happens about two months after the events pass. During years that things are quiet, I am reminded of previous events.

Close Your Eyes Little One

If you have ever had to subdue someone that you love, you know that this is not an easy task. Even when you know that it is for their good. When you have to help strap a loved one into a straight jacket, this is rough. To do this when you are holding a one year old is worse.

When Terry had a severe episode, I remember holding my youngest in my arms and going through these things. When we had him, she was fine for about 2 years. Then she had a very bad episode.

After sedating her, I filled out paperwork, I handed the baby to an officer. He looked at me, then the baby, and did not say a word. I knew in his expression, though, that he would not even consider exchanging places.

If you have never gone through these things, you do not know how I feel. For those of you who have, I pity you. The curse that has befallen you is beyond words. My teary eyes only hide the pain of the situation. To try to raise a family and deal with these things is sometimes impossible at best.

The only consolation that I have is that the youngest does not remember these things. Luckily he does not recall me helping strap Terry down and aid in sedating her. I guess in time, when he reads this, he will know. Until then, I will try to shield him.

"How do we know our place and ability, if
we never have struggled so hard?
A bead of sweat only shows the effort, but
the pain determines the cost."

The Balance of Things

15 Aug

Joy and sadness go hand in hand. The tears shall balance out.
A laugh and a cry shall equal peace. Nature will keep the realm.

As the pendulum sways right, it must swing left. All that goes up will come down. A bad thought intended will somehow be good, in action or desire.

A strength and a weakness woven together create a human character.
Flaws and traits define our souls enabling our unique fiber.

Things we must forever remember will always be lost in memories.
A picture taken will show an image. Yet all who were there think different.

In life our journey shall be preordained. Yet we find ourselves lost on the way. At our arrival we always think of the many things we have forgotten.

My words and thoughts shall make you think. The ideas are yours alone.
Forever keep sight of the unseen. It shall walk up right in front of you.

Kitchen Safari

To work in my kitchen is like going on a safari. You never know what you will find around any corner. Sometimes this makes the most mundane task interesting.

Cooking Dilemma

The most annoying aspect of this tendency is the relocation of cooking ware. When I am trying to cook I need a pot, pan or dish of some type. I go to the cabinet. It isn't there. I check the dishwasher, still no pot. I check the stove. She has a habit of putting dirty dishes in the oven. They are still not to be found. I get ready to give up. I look out the kitchen window. Low and behold, there is the dish in the back yard. I go out to get it and find 2 or 3 more that I haven't missed yet.

"Why did you put them outside?" I would ask. "To feed the animals," she would reply. That is as good an answer as any. It is hard to argue with that logic. I wish I had thought of that, I think to myself. I shake my head and continue with the cooking. I instruct the kids to keep an eye out for dishes while they're in the yard.

One important point I must make here. It is imperative to check the oven before turning it on. Normally this is a good practice anyway. In my house you will never know what you will find there. To find cardboard, food, dishes, or anything else does not surprise me.

Sometimes I find pots with food in them left in the oven. This drives me nuts. I don't know how long it has been there. She tells me she forgot about it. Then she'll put it in the refrigerator and tell me it is still good. This is a warped version of Russian roulette to me. I warn the kids and make a mental note not to eat it. When she isn't looking, I throw it out and say it was good.

Food

This is an amazing topic. It is an essential in life. However, the use or improper use is readily evident at times. The concept of an expiration date has apparently eluded her. Even though the packaging clearly defines the date when best used by, we still keep it around for years, just to make sure that it is bad before we throw it out.

It may be surprising to most, but to find an item that is five years beyond its date is normal. I touch nothing on the shelf that has not been put there recently. If it has dust on it, it is a clear sign that it has been around a while. If you do not recognize the item, or the packaging is so old that you have seen it on the auction channel, don't eat it.

I've thrown things out and been asked why. I tell her that Moses packaged it. She just gives me a look. I love it when she asks me to smell something to see if it is bad. I look at the date and see Lincoln was president when it was wrapped. I tell her that you can be sure that it is bad.

The chore of disposing of unknown food items usually falls to me. There are times when, with all of my science background, I am at a loss as to what the item was. It actually becomes a game.

Let's start with animal, vegetable or mineral. Could it have been meat at one time? Is it grown in a garden? Partial labels give it away too easy so I take them off. I only use them to cheat if I am stumped. If it is wrapped in foil, then all bets are off. There are times when she tells me what it was and I am amazed. It became this after starting out as that?

I especially enjoy getting rid of old fruits and vegetables. Let's see if we can make this melon collapse in on itself over time. Fruit flies need a condominium. Lets leave this out for weeks and see how many can live there. When I throw it out and she gives me a hard time, I just shake my head. I know—only the side that was down touching the table was bad. The rest of it was good, right? I just check the kitchen weekly; if I don't, then I am looking for trouble. I especially enjoy throwing bad items out my back door far into my rear yard or the woods and watch them explode when they hit the ground.

Cleaning Behind the Refrigerator

Another adventure unto itself is cleaning behind any appliance in the house. They are only cleaned when I can get to them. I have found many things there. Money, children's toys, pet's toys, clothing, and numerous other things that were given up for lost. As I pull out the appliance I cringe. I am not really sure that I want to do this, but I know that I have to.

It amazes me how she will have claimed to have cleaned the kitchen, but not moved anything. This is a baffling miracle to me. How can you clean when nothing is touched? I guess it qualifies as a miracle for the church or something. I am not sure. I wish that I could do that. I have to move things to clean. Luckily I have developed a liking to cleaning so it has never bothered me. It is one of the household chores that I like. She favors vacuuming. I like cleaning. It works.

We had a worker repairing something in the house. I know that behind the refrigerator had not been cleaned for a while. I remembered the last time that I did it. I was so embarrassed. We pulled it out and dust bunnies and other things were found. He said he had seen a lot worse. I still felt bad and cleaned it quickly before he got to work.

PINBALL WIZARD

Each of us has quirks and odd traits. Some, though, are very annoying. We tend to forget the things that we can deal with. We harp upon the things that we can't deal with. In any marriage there is give and take. Sometimes, though, you wonder who is giving and who is taking!

WHAT A DEAL

One day Terry came home with something. My father-in-law drove his truck up to our door and wanted to know where to put it. I asked a stupid question. "What, pray tell, what is it?" "A pinball machine, of course," he said. After giving him a blank look for a few moments, it became apparent to him that I had no idea what he was talking about.

We unloaded it onto our porch. It was very heavy and unyielding. I knew we were not going to move it far. I set it up there and decided to be brave and plug it in. It actually lit up. It didn't work right, but it wasn't dead. I turned the power off and decided to check it out.

It is funny how I recognized that machine. I had played one just like it as a kid years ago. I figured what the heck. I cleaned the relay contacts and we tried it again. This time it worked better. There were still problems, but I figured that.

At this point Terry realized that it might work all right. I told her that I was leery to try to repair it. The circuitry was very old. I had no schematics (electrical drawings) so I felt that it would probably be a great waste of my time. She wanted it repaired.

No House Call

We found an individual who repaired pinball machines in our area. He would not make a house call, though. So now we had to transport the machine over to his shop. The shop was about twenty miles away. It was an adventure to load this thing in the truck in two parts because of the weight. I secured it and off we drove to the shop.

When we arrived, I untied the ropes and unloaded it. In his shop he had a number of machines in various states of disrepair. Many were old machines that I remember playing on when I was growing up. They really brought back a lot of memories. There were pinball and arcade machines from years gone by. Some he even let us play and the kids had a good time. We left him our name and number and he said he would call back in a week or so and update us.

As we left his property, I saw old machines that had been parted out long ago. It was a literal graveyard of arcade memories. We drove away and awaited his call. Terry was happy and I just wondered what she had gotten me into again.

We went home and I walked around the house wondering what would happen next. I thought, "If this guy can actually fix that machine, what do I do? Am I the only one thinking where in the world are we going to put this?" I asked Terry and she just gave me a blank look. I knew this would be a matter for the future.

CPR Worked

The service man called us and told us that with a little work, he had repaired it. I was at the same time amazed and excited. He told us that we could pick it up at anytime. We decided to pick it up on a Saturday. We drove to his shop and he demonstrated it to us. The machine worked well.

It really brought back a lot of memories for me. That exact same machine was one that I had really enjoyed playing a kid. It was now about 28 years old, but worked. The cabinet was in very good shape and he told us it was worth a good deal of money. He asked what we had paid for it and we told him around $50.00. He was amazed and said in good working order it was worth around $500.00. If it worked, though, I did not want to sell it. I would rather let the kids play with it.

We carefully loaded the machine into our truck and headed back to the house. I tried to figure out where to put it the whole way home. I still really had no idea when we pulled into the driveway. I knew that she would want to play it, though. When we arrived home the discussion began. After a debate and discussion, we decided to bring it into the house.

New Piece of Furniture

Now that we decided to bring it into the house, which room should it go in? We discussed and decided that the only room that we could put it was the dining room. Moving it into that room would be a real treat. The machine was heavy, unyielding and not very easy to manipulate through the house. I backed up the truck and we proceeded to unload it again.

Memories from the last time that we had done this went through my head. At least this time, though, I knew about it. I also knew that it worked. That gave me added incentive to get it into the house. The last time, I wasn't so sure.

After wrestling with the machine and getting it through the front door, we struggled to get it into the dining room. It was a relief to put it down and take a break. I figured the one corner in the dining room was the best spot for it. It had an outlet and was generally out of the way.

I plugged the machine in and waited a little bit while I parked the truck and put away the ropes and cords we used to secure it. When I came in, we decided to turn it on and try it.

I looked over at the kids. Their eyes lit up and I could see the excitement in their faces. They waited and watched all of the lights and marveled at all of the sounds of the old mechanics going through the process of resetting themselves. It took a number of seconds for the machine to go through its process and prepare to be played.

There was a coin bank that came with it. It seemed senseless to me to use dimes and quarters to play it, though. I considered it as a way to make money, but reconsidered. We decided to disconnect that circuit and the mechanic showed us how to reset and add games to the counter. I opted for that function. I proceeded to set the counter for about twenty games and left Terry and kids to begin to play.

Any Ear Plugs Handy

I never realized how loud an old pinball machine actually was. As a kid, I had always played them in arcades or in stores. There was always so much background noise that

I never paid attention to the machine's noises. It amazed me that I could hear it from any room in the house.

Just by the sounds heard, I could tell who was playing it. My youngest always lost the ball rather quickly so I knew when he was playing. The oldest had a habit of slapping the side of the machine to jiggle the ball in the direction that he wanted. Occasionally he tilted the machine. Terry usually just operated the flippers with no shaking of the machine. That gave each one of them characteristic sounds that I learned to distinguish well. If I wanted to know who was playing, I would just put my ear to the wind and listen. Within a few seconds, I knew who was up. I also knew if there was more then one of them playing.

For a number of weeks the machine worked well and they played it up until far too late at night for me. It was Terry's pride and joy. She was so proud of herself. Even kids from the neighborhood came by and played it. I watched them and thought back to when I was their age. I could see wonderment in their eyes.

All Things Must Pass

One day while they were playing the counters and flippers stopped working right. I checked the relays and contacts, but told her she had to call the mechanic. We called and this time he made a house call. He came out the next week and worked on it. When he left it worked fine for about two weeks. Then it developed problems again. Terry was disappointed.

She called the mechanic back and he came one last time. He told her that it should be rebuilt due to some mechanical problems that he just couldn't adjust. She asked him for an estimate. When he gave her the price, she just looked at me. I could see the disappointment in her face. At this point I had supported her and been patient enough. I told her that the money would be better spent in a much newer machine without the mechanics. She wouldn't listen. I informed her that it was her decision. I wanted no part of it.

Today and Forever

Now comes the reason why I told you this story. Over the years I have learned that you have to choose your battles. There are times when it is best to say nothing and just walk away. That is what I have done in this case.

The conclusion of this story goes as follows.

The pinball machine has sat in my dining room for years now. It doesn't work. It hasn't been repaired. It collects dust, clothes, papers and many other assorted materials. Every day she swears she will get it fixed. She asks me when I will build a garage to put it in. I walk past it and shake my head. She will not sell it. I have found that when she attaches to an item, it is impossible for her to let go. I have fought her before on this subject and lost. The moral of the story is if you deal with these things on a daily basis, go fishing. You will live longer and be happier.

Seen Any Good Doll Heads Lately

Many comical things occur during these episodes. At least there are times when a good laugh is the best medicine when dealing with this. Some things go on well into the future. They become constant and ongoing events. Year round you deal with them and keep a sense of humor. This is one of those ongoing situations. It still brings a laugh to us all. A running joke that I hope keeps on running.

The Initial Dismemberment

At the peak of a severe episode, Terry decided to rearrange body parts on a doll that she had. This was an old doll that she had received when her grandmother had died. It was fully clothed the last time I had seen it.

She came down stairs with it in her hands and told me she was going to work on the doll. The next thing that I knew the legs and arms were off of the torso. She then reattached them, but not in the proper places. The clothes that had come with the doll were nowhere to be found.

Her next move was to remove the head. I thought this entertaining but did not say a word. I just sat back and watched the show. With the head off and the arms and legs in the wrong sockets, she decided to go outside. She carried the doll body in one hand and the head in another. A few moments later she returned with the head. It was attached on the end of a broom handle. The body was nowhere to be found.

Have Body Will Travel

The next day consisted of intense grilling for the location of the body. She did not have the head in her possession at this point. This quickly became a tennis match where one minute she had the head, and the next the body. Every time that the body reappeared, it changed. A leg was missing, or in an arm socket. An arm moved to a leg socket and both legs missing. On it went for the rest of the day. I watched this while trying not to laugh. This annoyed her when I did.

Finally she returned with just the head. I had not seen the body in hours. Maybe she had stowed the body? I didn't know. She was basically out of trouble. She was just entertaining herself and me.

I didn't think twice about it and continued working.

After this episode ended, she inquired about the doll. I had not seen it for a while. While cleaning in the attic later, I found the remnants of the body. All arms and legs were there, but not attached properly. I put them back in the right sockets and handed her the body. I had not seen the head, but figured she knew where it was.

Now she had the body. Where was the head? It was on the end of that broom handle the last time I had seen it. I looked for the head for a while, but gave up. I didn't find it. She went searching for it herself to no avail. A few years went by and I found the head. It was in an obscure box filled with clothes and other things. I informed her that I now had the head and I gave it to her. She took it and came back shortly claiming that she had no idea where the body was now.

Still Looking

To date, the doll is still dismembered. Every time I find one part, she loses the rest. It has become a running joke in the house. In fact, just recently she asked me if I had seen the body. Of course I had not.

I don't even bother looking for it. I'm sure the body wanders at night looking for its head. Good luck, I say. If I do find all of the parts, I will glue them all together, just to save myself aggravation in the future. If you find the doll, burn it. I think it is haunted.

By the way, she originally took the doll outside to hang it on a clothesline to let it dry.

Don't ask . . .

The Doll

18 Mar

In human form attached with care and parts are placed just so.
It is our nature to rearrange to suit the individual intended need.
The fact remains that God did the work to perfect his gifts to us.
Who do we think we are on earth, to change a natural thing?

With mind adrift in unknown place the thoughts of trouble bring.
We heed not warnings and given signs but stray apart from course.
When finished we look back to find our work is less than real.
But since we can't accept our faults we blame others for the acts.

Dismantled dolls are not just toys, but children that we raised.
We break them down to build up ourselves and toss the parts unused. Are
we so sure we are better builders with what we have created?
The shell relives our deeds and acts hopefully not to be renewed.

Most think themselves superior then. Better then the rest.
If truth be told, they destroyed and harmed the greatest things they had.
As aging occurs we become our parents in many ways and forms.
In lessons learned we shaped the clay, molded falsely in our youth.

Be kind and gentle to treasured gifts, our babies from days past.
In time they know how soft the words of love shall find their ears.
Mistakes will happen as we stumble through guardian adventures found.
Always know they forgive the pains of growth we all endure.

Vehicles and Illegal Parking in the Woods

One of my primary concerns about her episodes was the use of vehicles. Out of all of the times she took a car or truck in the middle of the night, she never once committed a traffic violation that I was aware of. I found this to be an amazing feat. If you had seen her drive normally, you would not argue. The other thing that amazes me is that she never ran out of gas. She always had sense enough to return while the vehicle had enough gas to get her home. You have no idea how many mornings I found ALL of the vehicles in my driveway on E. They were empty, but they were there.

Preventative Measures

As episodes occurred, I learned to control her wandering around with cars and trucks. I would intentionally disable them as not to let her drive them away. She did surprise me a few times and figured out what was wrong. She would repair it, and take the car. I was astonished by this and learned to disable them better.

The worst thing about her taking vehicles was that she would take them into places where they are not supposed to go. Many a time I had to go into the woods or elsewhere to retrieve vehicles that she had gotten stuck.

It never ceased to amaze me how well she handled vehicles. In her frame of mind, she could get a vehicle into places that no one else would ever manage. This occurred usually right before she was hospitalized. It allowed me time to retrieve and repair them before she would return home.

It was not always a bad thing, either. Since I knew she was going to do it—I could sense she had that frame of mind—I would intentionally leave only one vehicle in running order and disable the rest. I would usually leave the one car that I could afford to lose and did not care if she destroyed it. In this way I could control the damage she would inevitably inflict.

Seek and Find

The worst event involving a vehicle went like this.

One night she took one of our cars out. She did not return until morning. The car, however, was nowhere to be found. I asked her where it was. She informed me that she had left it in the woods. It broke down on her and she left it.

I asked her if she knew where it was. She informed me that she knew its location. She said I could drive her right to it. I grabbed tools and a flashlight. Even though it was against my better judgment, we set off to recover the car. This is one of those "should not have done it" moments that I will never forget.

Let's step back for a moment and recap this situation.

I am leaving the safety and comfort of my house to go into the woods with a crazy woman who says she knows where a car is. Does anybody else see a red flag flying here? I still went. Not one of my finer moments, I assure you.

We drove into the woods. When we reached the presumed area that the car was, we left the truck and walked a short distance down the dirt road. The car was supposedly a short walk from that intersection. I stayed by the truck with my youngest, who was a baby. I instructed the oldest to go around the bend, survey the situation, and then come right back.

Of course you can guess he did no such thing. He walked down the road with Terry and disappeared into the sunset. I called out at the top of my lungs. I received no response. Now I was worried. I gave them thirty minutes.

After the thirty minutes, I wrote a quick note and attached it to the tree where the truck was. I called out again. No one responded. I decided that it was time to get help.

I drove back down the road to a campground and talked to the owner. I informed him that Terry and son were lost in the woods, and gave him an approximate position. I told him that I was going to return to that departure spot and wait. He called the park service.

A ranger showed up a short time later and I instructed him as to the direction and time of their departure. He informed me of the road that they were on and said he would investigate. In the mean time a second ranger appeared and stationed himself with me.

For two hours the rangers searched the woods, but did not find Terry or son. I was really starting to worry now. As luck would have it though, we received a call from the state police. They had found them and had taken them to the state police barracks.

I thanked the rangers and filled out the paperwork that was required. I drove to the barracks and talked to the desk sergeant. He informed me that they had found them walking down the road.

They had apparently wandered out onto a major highway. The police had then picked them up.

I arrived at the barracks, filled out the paperwork, and drove them home. The officers asked me if things were okay. I said, "No, but what can I do?" They knew something was wrong, but no laws were broken. After six hours, and excessive worrying, I returned home.

You are probably wondering where the car is. I will tell you. It was still in the same spot that it was when this all had started. I had come full circle. I called it a day and decided to deal with the rangers in the morning.

In the morning, I drove to the local ranger station. I just mentioned the recent events and they knew exactly what I was talking about. I informed them that Terry had broken down and left her car in the woods, and that is what had started the whole scenario. I also told them I was not sure of the exact location of the car. They said they would look for the car and get back to me.

The rangers found her car the next day. This was with the assistance of three park rangers and the state police. Upon discovery, the ranger asked me how the vehicle ended up where it was. I told him not to ask.

Apparently Terry drove the vehicle off state property and onto federal land. This in itself was not a major issue. She did, however, drive the car onto a Military Range. The car was broken down on the fringes of the property.

I filled out the necessary paperwork and proceeded to the vehicle. Upon arrival, I inspected the car. She had left it with the keys in the ignition, the doors and trunk open, and all of the contents strewn about in a large circle. It had amazed me that all of the belongings were still there. I especially worried about a tackle box of mine that she had taken. She thought it was a tool box.

I packed all of the possessions up and started to figure out how to get it out of there. To my amazement, they were worried that the vehicle was blocking the dirt road that it was left on. I wondered why, if it had taken them two days to locate it, would they be concerned with traffic flow?

It was one of those times that I did not see the sense in arguing. I spent my Saturday attempting to remove it. When I had received the call that they had found it, it had snowed. It took me 4 hours, lots of patience and a few prayers to get it out.

By the way, the reason that it broke down on her was that she drove through a large puddle and stalled it out. I dried off the cap and wires and other electrical parts. I somewhat started the car up. The problem now was the sandy soil. I was the only driver there. I had brought my tow bar and decided just to tow it home. I junked the car shortly afterward.

Yearly Bits of Rage

There are times when I don't understand the anger. When they occur, I think it is a venting process. It is her way of letting off steam. Each of us has ways of getting rid of our anger. This is usually a healthy activity.

There are times when I think that it tends to go overboard. She will overreact to a situation and really let loose. Most of the time I just let it go and take into account pressures or strains. A few times, though, I have to step in and try to get things under control.

Hot Dogs and Cheese

On one afternoon I was sitting at my computer working on a paper when all of a sudden I heard a scream. I then heard lots of yelling and ranting. Terry walked into the room where I was and began yelling at me. She spoke of how she bought food and I was expected to eat it. I just gave her a puzzled look. This infuriated her more.

She then lifted up a block of cheese and a pack of hot dogs and asked me if I would eat these. I gave her a confused look and asked what she was talking about. She again asked if I would I eat these. She showed me the hot dogs and cheese again. I said, "I guess, but not right now. I'm not hungry."

Apparently my oldest had questioned the expiration dates on the packages and this aggravated her. I calmed her down and told her that I would eat them at the appropriate time. This made her feel better and she went back to other things.

Empty Threats

Many times I find that she will threaten me to get me to do things that she wants me to. She will tell me that she will do something stupid to make me pay. If she doesn't get her way this occurs more often. I usually just let her complain. It is her way of trying to control situations. It is very rare when she carries through with any of her threats.

When I don't succumb, she pulls a 180-degree turn and approaches it from the opposite direction. She is usually very nice to me and tries that approach. I normally see right through it and just pay her no mind. Eventually she goes back to her normal self and all is well.

If all else fails she begins to ask why I don't love her. We start the dance of wills that inevitably ends up in failure for both of us. The "You don't love me, you don't care" argument goes nowhere. Neither is true. I just don't bother to argue the point.

Suicide Threats

This subject is the most troublesome of all. Any threat of suicide has to be taken seriously. Even when I think she is just joking around, the thought is always in the back of my mind. I immediately go on suicide watch and monitor her even more closely than normal. She has never attempted it to my knowledge. It only takes one time to succeed, though.

Suicide threats have occurred sporadically. I check her tone and mood to determine how serious she is. Normally she is just upset about something and all that I need to do is watch her.

These events pass without any major problems or concerns. On rare instances, I have had to react, though.

Kids and Anger

When raising kids, they will eventually get to you. In times of stress they do things without thinking about the consequences. I have seen them push buttons with her and then regret it. I try to referee, but I can't be around all of the time.

Any anger towards the kids is my primary concern. She is usually a good mother, but there are times when she overreacts. I stop her and try to keep the peace in the house. I have seen the oldest intentionally egg her on and then look surprised when things blow up in his face. She knows that boys will be boys and their behavior leaves a little to be desired. When she is in sensitive times, they are usually behaved. As with any children, they do things that they shouldn't and pay for it.

The worst part of her anger is when she takes things of mine to try to control me. She will take something that I need. I have found that I should just tell her to keep it. It usually diffuses the situation. When she gets upset or annoyed it happens. I then try to figure out what started the problem. Usually it is something silly that turned into a misunderstanding.

Final Curtain

"The greatest achievements that we manage are always created from a series of simple acts combined in such a way as to enable the conquering."

Feelings

There were times when I found that I still had feelings and cared for her. Other times I couldn't stand being in the same room with her. This juggling act that had occurred was annoying. One minute I thought we could be civil, the next I would want to run.

Feelings are the hardest part of all of this, especially for a guy. It is hard enough to deal with all the rest. When you don't understand why and how you feel, it is nearly impossible at times. The struggle to figure out control and handle what happens taxes your every nerve.

I constantly talk to friends and have them explain these things to me. They have a much keener awareness. I often have no idea and need them to tell me why, how or what is going on. Usually they can shed light and help me adjust to the changes. At least it makes me feel a little bit better to understand it.

Sometimes I have no clue what they are talking about and just tilt my head to one side like a puppy hearing a strange sound. They just shake their heads at me and laugh. That is when I know I am in trouble. There is nothing worse than to be at their complete mercy. They have me where they want me. I just hope that I haven't annoyed them in a while. They will make me pay.

You Can't Leave

During one of our many discussions about divorce, Terry told me that I couldn't leave. I just shook my head at her. She continued by saying that if I did leave, she would commit suicide. I looked at her and knew that she was probably upset and just saying that. I knew she wasn't in an episode, but the stress might make her do something she would regret.

I had no intent of leaving that day, so I avoided the conversation and brought up something else to get her mind off of it. This statement is very powerful and bothers me. It is a tool that she has used in the past to sway my judgment. Before, I was not well. It worked every time. Now, though, I see how it is a better reason to leave. To say that to someone means that you have no concept of true relationships.

The Final Decision

The final decision on separation had taken me well over a year to make. I thought and debated the whole affair. I knew the impact on myself and my family. It was not an easy act. It was probably the most difficult decision in my life. When you have children it is compounded.

One morning I woke up with a clear head and just made the decision. I realized that my current life was not what

I wanted or deserved. I decided a "Thelma and Louis" act was necessary. I was going to hit the gas and take my chances.

The security of staying there was doing more damage than good. With that, I proceeded to make arrangements and start a life outside of the prison I had called a home for many years. The sun came out that day from behind the thick clouds that had enveloped it many years ago.

Many thoughts ran through my head. I thought about other couples I knew. I thought how others I had seen treat each other. I thought about how I felt I was fundamentally missing something in my life.

I hated walking through the lunch room at work while people sat and ate. I would hear people complain how their wife or girlfriend didn't cook something for them or forgot to throw something in their lunch that day. The apple has a spot, the bread is soggy, and where are the crackers? I envied every one of them . . .

I realized that none of them really understood how good they had it. I would listen and shake my head. It is hard for someone who is used to someone caring for them in a loving way to understand. I equate it to standing in front of a starving person with a bag of groceries. To you they are just simple groceries. To them, they are a grand feast beyond measure.

Sometimes people really can't see the forest through the trees. It just depends on your perspective, I guess.

Reasons for Leaving

Here is a list of reasons for leaving. This is only a general list and I could add much more. After many years I realized I had to do this. It was not worth the toll it was taking on me.

In the last year of marriage, after I started to attend counseling again, I realized that I had subjected myself to things that were not necessary. Although you learn to tolerate things just for peace, it becomes too much and you eventually have enough.

All that I ever wanted was an equal relationship. The work involved to keep this going was just not worth what I was getting out of it. I did not hate or dislike Terry; I became indifferent to her. I just felt I could find someone else who would treat me the way I wanted to be treated.

Below is a list of some of the things that were happening. It is not the entire list, but there are enough things here for you to get an idea. All that I basically ever wanted was to be loved and appreciated. Nothing fancy, just simple.

This is a partial list that pushed me to leave. That sounds kind of funny considering what I had been through up to this point. I suppose a normal person would not have come this far.

For instance:

- I had asked Terry not to hit anymore. She would say that I deserved it and that is why it happened. She stopped doing this eventually.

- I asked her for many months to go to counseling. Everyday for over six months she refused. I gave up. She would tell me she was not ready for it. As I was leaving she conceded to counseling. I didn't care at that point. If you ask someone for help for over six months, when you are walking out who cares what they say.

- She blamed me for her institutionalizations.

This really bothered me. I didn't do anything to her. I protected her as best as I knew how. I didn't cause it and I helped anyway I could. Blame here wasn't fair at all.

• She would take my car keys and ID's to prevent me from leaving the house or going to work.

• She would block the front and rear doors and try to stop me from leaving the house.

• If I packed a bag of clothes to leave she would take the bag and all of the clothes and forbid me to leave. "You can't leave. I won't allow it," she would say.

• I was not allowed to go over the house of family I had in the area without her permission.

• I was told by her that since we were married that meant she could do anything she wanted to me.

• I was the one not taking my marriage vows seriously.

That completes a pretty good list for not wanting to come home. I still went home after work to protect the kids and to keep an eye on things. I hated entering the house. I did it anyway.

Things did not get to that point overnight, though. A gradual progression of me allowing behavior is what had occurred. That is how I see it. Now I stop it abruptly. Once I see issues and problems, I end it there.

That is all part of what I said before. We cause our own dilemmas more often than not. I do not fault her for being her. I fault me for not taking control of my own life and ending things sooner.

Separated

Eventually, I knew there was no turning back. I had to leave. This is where the story turns around. I packed some things in a bag and tried to walk out the door. I honestly wasn't sure of where I was going to go but didn't care. I knew I had to get out.

When she saw me leaving she grabbed the bag and said, "You can't leave. I won't allow it." She took my things and ran upstairs. I was ready to argue but decided another time may be best. I decided that leaving with her present wasn't going to work.

I decided the best thing to do was to work on a place to go and then when I had that set, I could leave. That is what I concentrated on. It was hard but I knew I had to. It is funny to be so unsure and sure at the same time, a confusing situation.

Once I had a place for myself I planned on leaving when I knew she wouldn't be home. I told her the night before I was leaving and she didn't believe me. I packed some of my things and left in the morning. It was an amazing feeling. The first breath I had taken in years. Friends couldn't believe I actually did it. I said I felt like the Janis Joplin lyrics in the song Bobby McGee. "Freedom is another word for nothing left to lose."

As I drove down the street, the theme from mission impossible played in my head. Poetic justice, don't you think? When I arrived at my new place I started to unpack what I had brought. It felt so good. A short time later I received a phone call from the police.

They wanted to know the condition of my kids. Terry had reported them kidnapped. She told the police I had taken my kids out of the country without her permission. The older laughed at the police officer's suggestion. This really didn't surprise me.

Settling of Contents

I arrived at my place and couldn't believe it. I had left. I had done what I never thought I would do. I look back now and pat myself on the back. Friends have told me how much courage I must have had to do it. I uprooted myself and my kids. I walked away from what I knew as wrong. You know what is really funny? I don't think it took courage. I think it was more of a survival instinct.

Once I finished unpacking I sat down and rested in the grass. I realized how much my life had changed that morning. For those of you who have never experienced these kinds of things let me describe it this way: It is the equivalent of staying under water for as long as you possibly can. At the last second you decide to go up for a breath of air. You just get to the surface when your body is forced to breathe. You feel a rush of oxygen flow through you. You sense the crisp, clean air flare your nostrils and cleanse the soul. You are happy to be alive. You feel newly alive and are grateful for that life.

Even though I had chosen my direction, I still felt lost and scared and lonely. After being with someone else for so long, I was now alone. I had rolled the dice. The number still wasn't clear to me. It didn't matter. There was no turning back.

The legal implications of all of this were just starting and I knew I had to deal with that. I expected a long, ugly fight. I also knew in the end I would find life again. My senses had told me I did the right thing. The other aspect being at this point I was mentally and physically drained. I needed to rest, regroup, and heal. The healing process was underway. I needed my space.

I was only in the new place a short time when I wrote a poem.

Face of God

June 21

In the wind-swept ripples of the water I see the face of God.
Old and wrinkled, yet wise beyond all years.
Each line a mark of passing. Each rise of water a victory of justice.
Forever quiet, but shouting to the heavens.
Look at me. I am your path.
You become mesmerized and entranced.
All of the things wrong in this world become trivial.
Peace reigns in your mind and heart.
As the winds die down you are released.
You go back into the world refreshed and enlightened.

Most people don't know the face of God.
They have never taken the time to look upon him in his simplicity.
That is where he resides.
Cast upon the surface of lakes and ponds.
In the faces of innocent children.
In the starry moonlit night.
In the bark of an old oak tree.
In all of the places that no one ever bothers to look.
He is there.

It was a simple poem. However, to me, it was my path. I knew I was supposed to write. I felt it. Whenever I tried to write in the past, I would be accused, interrupted or distracted. Now I had the peace and quiet to do it.

I could write poems or stories or anything I wanted to

express myself; a rebirth of sorts. Since that time I have written constantly. It is something that I enjoy and I have included some poems throughout this work.

Deep Breath

The benefits of moving out were immeasurable. Up until that point I could not sleep. I was not eating right. I suffered from headaches and fatigue and cried every day. I was told that medication would help, but since I am stubborn I decided to handle things on my own.

Once I was away, though, I gradually began to sleep more. My sleep went from 3 hours daily to over 6 hours. That was a monumental change. I started to eat properly and actually gained a couple of pounds. I had had trouble maintaining my weight up until that point. My headaches went away and the crying subsided to only an occasional event. I felt better, stronger and more alert. I began doing things that I loved again. I appreciated life.

The next thing that happened was I began to make friends and socialize a little bit. Although I was always shy, I liked being around certain individuals. I had been dealing with things so long that I felt so out of place at any social event it really bothered me. I struggled at the first gatherings but eventually began to fit in. I am quiet by nature.

Adjustment Period

As with any change in arrangement there is an adjustment period. I liked the fact of the quiet and time to write and just reflect. I started to feel better. I had to still deal with the one aspect that I knew would haunt me, the ex adjusting to the separation.

At first it was hard for me to begin to separate myself entirely. I knew that after many years we both had to come to terms with all of this. It is not an easy thing to do. Her constant pleas and cries for help wore thin fast and I grew tired. She constantly wanted to know about herself and how I would make things better for her. That is the stance I expected from her. I just wanted to be left alone.

There is a fact that everyone must accept. The world is full of givers and takers. All in the world must be one or the other. I wasn't a taker. I didn't want anything. I didn't ask for anything. I expected nothing of no one. I just wanted to give my love to someone who would appreciate it. It was a simple request, really; just very difficult to bring to fruition.

I had to teach myself not to go to the ex's aid and not to believe that it was my responsibility to rescue her from things. She would have to make it on her own. My responsibility was waning and I was going to have to let go myself. That sounds easy but isn't. Being a caretaker for so long lent itself to me being helpful and supportive. I had a hard time mustering up the word no.

Things in the past that I always believed myself to be responsible for were no longer my jobs. I finished some things up that I had started around the house and left.

I hated even entering that house. Every room, every hallway had memories for me. Events occurred everywhere. Memories were conjured up around every corner. The sights and sounds at times still came back to me. The house had a "smell" that I sensed and disliked. It had an essence and tragic aura. Too much pain encased in its walls.

I had my own place to try to get up and running and functional. I took virtually nothing with me but was accused of removing everything. I thought that was amusing. I had no money to speak of and no belongings, short of what I carried in a couple of boxes. I left with what little I thought was rightfully mine. All the furniture, household items, and other contents were left intact.

Roughing It

For weeks I slept on the floor in the back bedroom. I didn't have the money for a bed. I didn't care. I decided I'd rather sleep on the floor there on my own than in a bed in the other house. I had no furniture, no phone, no cable, minimal lighting and no kitchen utensils. Still, I was determined to make it.

I started by getting furniture for the kids' rooms. I picked up beds and dressers for them. That was a start. I was used to sleeping in a sleeping bag anyway. The next thing was kitchen utensils. I gathered pots and pans and dishes and anything else I could be given or purchased.

I then splurged and picked up a coffeemaker, toaster and microwave. The kitchen was set.

I started to cook regular meals again and it felt good. Although I was still mentally exhausted, I was feeling better. Between work and home, my life was busy.

Little things around the house came gradually. Friends and family gave me things and I was grateful. I never minded doing without. I never had much to begin with and never was a material person. I had my pen and paper. I had simple things that made me happy. I had my peace of mind. That held more value than everything I had ever bought in my life.

My daily therapy was simple. I burned a candle on the mantelpiece everyday and watched the flame. It lit up my living room. I didn't have a lamp but didn't care. I learned how natural lighting calmed me and I reflected and meditated as I viewed it. The flame was mesmerizing. I would sit and watch it dance. It swayed and gently moved in the breeze. Its motion and grace reminded me of an elegant ballerina practicing her craft. The light gave the room a soft appearance and soothed my soul.

So it went on for months. I gathered things gradually and made specific things priorities. Other things had to wait. I needed nothing, really, except enough food for us and utilities. We had some clothes and the rest we were gradually acquiring. We were not poor. We were just starting all over again.

Initial Custody

I tried all of the time to keep the youngest by me but fought with the ex for a fair share. She would argue and inform me that as mother she had all the rights. I had an argument with a police officer one day. He said without a court order it is a free-for-all. I pushed my attorney to get us into court and get a visitation schedule in writing. That is what I did.

I held joint custody. I refused to relinquish my 50% custody rights. Even with her past, that is how it was. I had to approach the problem as cautiously as possible. To minimize strain on the youngest, I decided to handle it this way.

The mental illness angle is a double-edged sword. They have a little sympathy towards any of us for it. Step light and guard well. That is what I planned. A change in custody status would have to wait. It would take therapists, counselors, and a lot of time and money for that. Add to that the probing of the youngest and I decided I'd rather just steer a course and wait. If nothing happened, great. If something did happen, I was ready.

I tried to exchange the youngest as quietly as possible with her. When she would act up, though, the youngest was always made upset. It wasn't fair. He was just trying to be a child. None of this was his fault. He was a victim.

The worst aspect of the custody and visitation was the handling of our youngest. She would place the child in the middle and say that he didn't want this. I knew that. I honestly didn't either but couldn't live like that anymore.

A child doesn't belong in the middle of two adults discussing things. I never placed them there. She used them as a tool, which really bothered me. It was cruel and mean and bordered abusive in my eyes. That is only my opinion. I am not an authority there.

I wrote a poem about one incident that I witnessed. After I saw the treatment and behavior toward the youngest, these words just flowed.

Dark Dance

25 Aug

Unspoken grips and silent glides. Words are never needed.
Embraced and repulsed equally. Distance kept abreast.

Void of feeling, while intent is real. The motions say it all.
For in this dance a serious act. Humanity takes the fall.

A tear in the eye separates partners thus. For he sheds not one for thee.
A grin or a smile depicts his stance, as evil is blind you see.

Righteous strength with character are sharp weapons to be used.
He counters with indifferent care, senseless cruelty is abused.

The damage done is limitless, the pain beyond compare.
The tears act as measures of effectiveness, marks of triumph if you dare.

Most know not of the dance I speak. Quietly commenced upon each day.
Behind the scenes but very real, in God's and Satan's way.

Those of us who participate, we speak not of its tune.
We mention not of the melody, screams of fallen who are doomed.

A lack of understanding is a good thing here you see.
You know not of any of this. Ignorance filled with glee.

I leave you here to wonder. Think about and absorb.
Some of us have our dance cards full, while the rest wait at the door.

He always will look for partners. Keep your card tucked neat away.
Remember of the dance, that I spoke of here today.

Be grateful of the silence that surrounds you through the day.
Forget not those who hear the sounds, when darkness comes your way.

Although I wanted to call the youngest everyday he wasn't with me, I dreaded the phone conversations with the ex. I would talk to him for a few minutes and argue with her for half an hour. Even after I would hang up, she would call me back a number of times.

As things progressed in our separation I wanted less and less time around her. Eventually it became a chore to go around her. I had seen my feelings swing drastically away from her. This time, though, they would never swing back. I knew how and what I felt. At this point I wanted and needed my space.

Every morning I had cried on the way to work or in the shower. It was a very good release. As I was separated the crying occurred less every day. I felt the cleansing was very good for my soul. As it subsided it only came about when I wrote things or when I reflected back on what I had written earlier. It made editing very difficult. I learned to only read what I had to.

The good news here is it inspired me to write poetry. That was a very good release. It allowed quick, rather to the point releases of emotions and energy. It was draining and uplifting at the same time. The more that I wrote them the better I felt. I noticed how short bursts soothed the surges while long, drawn-out writing such as this drained me.

Restraining Order

One night I had enough of the comments and insinuations on the phone. I had my fill of the badgering and insults. I did not lower myself to that level and made sure not to speak negatively about her to the youngest. I held my opinion, although I would have loved to let both barrels fly.

After a series of phone calls and redials I told her I was getting a restraining order against her. She told me I had no right. That made me march quicker. It is bad enough to take it. It is worse to hear that you have no choice and you must take it because they say so.

With a short trip to the local police station I found myself filling out forms and speaking to officers. I had never envisioned myself doing this but knew I had to. If I was to have any peace it had to happen.

I explained my position to the officers and informed them I just wanted the harassment to stop. I understood at times she was upset, but knew that I had to get some peace. I had endured enough. The gloves were starting to come off. After the discussions and forms, the officer called a judge and I spoke with him. He was very nice and asked me to explain my situation and problem. After a little bit he said he would grant a temporary restraining order and that I would be required to go to court to secure a permanent order. That was fine with me.

I waited for a little bit while the officer filled out the paperwork and received my copies. We discussed the nature of the order and its implications. I thanked him and agreed to show up at court on the appointed day. He informed me that Terry would be served shortly and from then on, no contact could be made between us. That may sound cruel but to me it was a blessing. I would experience peace for a week. After years of noise, silence enveloped me. I liked it.

I went back home and as I entered the door the phone rang. I looked at the caller ID and it was her. I thought about laughing but just ignored the rings. It stopped and I went to bed. In the morning, I explained to the oldest what I had done. I then informed him why (which he knew already). The next day, I was informed that she was served.

So began my experience with silence. I enjoyed the fact that I could sit and read or watch TV without phone calls. Her record number of calls for a day had reached 18. Between cell phone and house calls, it had gotten out of hand.

The weirdest part about the whole matter was that although others had been telling me to do it, I didn't feel right about it. It would take a barrage to push me over the edge. The words "You don't have the right" were the right combination as well. If I was going to go down, I would make sure it would be in flames.

To Court We Go

Upon arriving at court, we were immediately separated in groups. It seems Domestic Violence (which is what this was construed as) breaks the parties into Plaintiff and Defendant sections. I found it interesting that I was the only male in the plaintiff section. Accordingly so, she was the only female in the defendant section.

I looked around the room to realize how my situation was strikingly different from all others. Judges are always viewing these matters in a rather standard way. I brought to the table a much different scenario. I understood why, at times, I felt my side was overlooked. It was not intentional, but general practice dictated for the protection of the female. As our case was called, I stood where no other male had that day. I was the one defending my rights.

Considering what I had been through up until then, it was kind of poetic. I had always ventured onto unspoken ground through what I had seen. I had endured many things in the past, so why should it not be me who stood there? Who better to represent the case?

The judge asked me why I thought a restraining order was necessary. He then listened to my story. After I completed speaking he asked Terry to explain her position. She spoke for a while and he asked her a few questions. She informed the judge that she did make a number of calls, but they were only to speak to my son.

When he turned back to me I said she would start speaking to him, but then direct the badgering at me. I informed him that I just wanted her to stop calling me. I also said her visits to my house and work should stop. He agreed.

It was never the fact that she called. It was the number of times and the tone of the conversations. I did not leave her to be treated that way elsewhere. I began to assert my belief that I deserved to be treated better. It was not my place to take it anymore. So I stood up. I was heard.

The judge ruled that the restraining order should be made permanent. That was a good answer to me. Contact was to be in writing only. She could not call my cell or work. She could not go to my house or work. That sounded great. I hated when she showed up at my work. It always created a nuisance and scene. It would mean she would be arrested for it now. For the first time I received the only thing I asked for. Peace.

At this point she argued with the judge and said she would appeal the whole matter. He wished her luck. I wasn't asking for anything great, just a chance to live again. That little sliver of life that I thought I deserved. It appeared to be too much to her, though. That told me right away I had done the right thing.

I left the court room in a much better mood. I realized that this victory would spell my release from captivity. For once I could walk and breathe. I didn't have to explain where I was or what I was doing. Even though I had been separated for six months, it had only felt like two weeks. Now I could get a chance at healing and getting back strength.

As I walked outside the sun was bright and the air was clean. My head was clear and my heart was high. I received a call shortly afterward that one of my recent poems had been read to everyone at work and mounted on a wall. Things were finally looking up. I had hope in my heart and pride in my soul. I had gone in the lions den and walked out with a carcass in my hands.

The first victory I had encountered in a long time. The battle had begun and the war was waged.

The Aftermath

The joy of quiet soon set in. A phone from her meant I didn't have to talk to her. She would start on the kids, though. The youngest would look for someone to hand the phone off to. The oldest would take the phone and after a little conversation hang up. That told me it wasn't me. He informed me that if she kept it up, he would get an order against her as well.

If I called her house she would allegedly have to go and get my child. She couldn't argue or try to talk to me about us. I would just tell her she was defying the court order and to please put my child on the phone. That was sometimes enough to persuade her to do it.

At times, she would get on another extension and start to badger and talk to me when I was on the phone with them. I told her to get off. She refused and insisted on the insults. I told her I was calling the police and hung up.

A few minutes passed and the children called back in tears. She had told them mommy would be put in jail and it was daddy's fault. The use of a child in that way disturbs me so. I constantly reassure them how I love them and none of this is their fault. Unfortunately, that is all that I can do.

I wrote a poem after certain events unfolded. It was my way of saying I was sorry for everything that was happening. Someday I hope the kids understand why I did things.

Forgive

Dec 6

With words and actions as fleeting times, life is a blur gone by.
We steer and run a crooked course no matter how we try.
As age and effort pass us by the emotion falls away.
Until at last it catches up on this our final day.

Lack of expression chokes my throat. It cuts off air, you see.
For little ones do not understand the grief consumed by me.
I hide and fight and find the stance that suits a position well.
But times and struggle can be overlooked as engulfed from flames from hell.

My child, please do not fear the look upon my face.
It captures for all time the mood of my heartfelt embrace.
I ask only this from you so young who know not of the strife.
Play well and hard and keep it real at so young in your life.

Forgive the elders for what they do. They know not their intent.
Your wonders glance and look with despair at all the actions sent.
Understand that they make best of mistakes and the trauma so.
They cry and tear of any approach for things you do not know.

You are not to blame or be confused in any and all effect.

You had not things involved with it. You were distant with neglect.
With fight and feud and argument you see what can't be told.
Though adults look at child thus, dear moments do unfold.

Regret and agony consume us now. We do what must be done.
Some day we hope you understand that it was God's will my son.
Keep toy and love close to your heart and someday it shall all pass.
For in the spring a blossom comes with rebirth of the mass.

I know you fear at all unsure the times as they commence.
Yet understand it will improve as effort's clear suspense.
The sun shall shine another day although it seems so far.
Look up not down upon your life and beam as if a star.

The care and love surrounding you may be disguised today.
But it is there in truest form and will never leave, just stay.
So finish all of your games my dear and give not thought again.
Take youth and life and best of times and hold them close as friend.

You would think that over time the restraining order would become less of a situation. However, it is a protective tool that is used when needed. There have been far too many events and situations in the past to discard it.

Child Transfers

One morning we were supposed to transfer our youngest between us and each get on our ways. The judge had said for us to institute curbside pickups. I obliged and picked them up as ordered. However, when the transfer involved coming to my house, things changed.

I was in the house and awaiting her arrival. Instead of just stopping by the curb, she pulled into my driveway. I made sure all belongings were gathered. After a kiss and a hug, I sent our youngest out to meet her. I thought that would end it. I began to clean around the kitchen but noticed that she had not left. I figured maybe they were talking and just went back to chores.

A little while later they were still there. I opened my side door and a conversation began. I tolerated the direction, language and tone and just asked her to leave. She refused. I informed her she now had our child. It was her day and time to spend with him. She ignored me and proceeded to beg me to come in the house. I refused and repeatedly asked her to leave.

You would think this would only go on for a short time. Well you would be quite wrong. After an hour and a half, it was still occurring. I decided that if she would plant herself in my driveway, then I would get some things done around my house. In ignoring her, I thought she would grow tired of the whole affair and go away. Just for good measure I would ask her to leave every few minutes.

The mistake I made, though, was turning my back to her. I entered my shed and proceeded to collect tools for work around the house. She came up behind me and blocked the door. I asked her to move so I could get work done. She refused and then grabbed me.

At this point I knew she wouldn't listen to me. I asked her to release me and leave. She refused. She wanted me to give her affection. I asked her again to let go and leave me alone. She refused. I had had enough. I moved toward the door with her grasping me and broke apart her hands from around me. I walked quickly to my house and entered the back door. I locked it and called the police.

I meant business. I had put up with her behavior for over an hour and a half. I had had enough. The 911 operator dispatched a police car and when the police arrived, they found her in my driveway. I followed the instructions of the operator and awaited contact with the police.

When the police knocked, I opened the door and let

two officers into my home. We spoke for a little bit and they asked about the current restraining order. I said I had an FRO (Final Restraining Order) and she violated it constantly but I just tolerated most annoying behavior. This was out of hand. I wanted her off my property. They obliged. I didn't file a complaint at that time. I didn't want her arrested in front of our child if I could help it.

At that point the police escorted her off of the property and informed me of my right to press charges against her. I would think about it. To be honest I had no real intent to pursue criminal charges. That all changed over the next day and a half with her tone and language to me. I was blamed for the fact our child was upset. Again it was my fault that I called the police.

Okay, now please explain to me how I didn't violate court orders, I didn't trespass, I didn't grab another human being against their wishes, I didn't attempt to trap another human being against his wishes. Yet, it was MY entire fault. Is there a pattern here?

That cemented to me the reason for the restraining order. Yet lawyers said to me they didn't feel the order was justified because I wasn't being beaten or "abused"? I find the funny thing with that is they themselves can't control her. Maybe I wasn't entirely right in what I had done. I knew, though, that I wasn't even close to being wrong.

I always thought in the back of my head that if I were a woman no one would even question my actions or the restraining order. However, being a guy, I was supposed to take this. Why? It affected me and it affected my kids. I thought justice was equal for all. I guess maybe not, huh?

Laws are implemented for the good of all. Laws are enforced to keep order. In a nutshell that is all I wanted. I don't bother you, you don't bother me. Sounds simple, right? I put up and ignore everyday. I take the high road and just keep going. Yet I am supposed to take behavior that is in no one's best interest. How can people change if they are never held accountable for their actions?

Court Again

The first time she was brought into court for violation of the restraining order, I was just sent a letter and her attorney had her plead guilty. With a fine and a slap on the hand she was told not to do it again. That sounds great. Justice is served and all are happy. Not exactly.

I thought maybe the act of going to court may dissuade her from attempting these actions again. I thought maybe I would be left alone because she had learned her lesson. Wishful thinking on my part.

Court just made her mad. How dare I stand up and say she was violating this order. After this conviction, the restraining order had to go. Her lawyer said that it wasn't fair and it should be under a civil order and not a criminal one. I thought about it but decided to wait it. My point was if nothing else happened, what was the concern? Her attorney had fears of her behavior. He didn't want her jailed.

Now explain how on one hand you are concerned about her behavior—you worry that a criminal act may occur and it bothers you how your client will act—all the while you are defending her and speaking on her behalf in court. Justice confuses me sometimes. How can you be right and wrong at the same time?

Round 2 in Court

Our second trip into court was a little different. With a second conviction of violation of the restraining order, jail time would be imposed, 10 days in jail if found guilty. Again I was perceived as the bad guy. I really felt she had crossed the line and had to learn. Every day I would tell her things were over between us. She didn't listen. I suppose that is my fault?

Incidents have happened since. I find it fascinating.

As we went through all of this the holidays approached. The seasons were entirely different from anything else we had encountered. We were a divided family being around each other part time. I still felt I had done the right thing. The phone calls started to wane but I was looked down upon by family for the entire matter. When you are outnumbered, remember one thing: Do what you think is right for you and the rest will follow.

I stood firm and alone. That is what they feared. I was willing to take any one of them on. They said things. I didn't. They made accusations that they knew were false. I didn't. They lied and falsely accused me. I stood in front of them and said bring it on. In court I won every time. I blew their garbage out of the water. Sure, they wouldn't talk to me. Then again, they would deny all of the problems throughout their lives. Why admit to anything now?

Holidays

Dec 20

A gift or card placed at the door. A present wrapped just so.
A thought or motion in loving response with those we think and know. At times the warmth envelopes us as others live in mind.
Upon our dreams they swim and float as memories of the kind.

Did you think a gift is overlooked because of cost or worth?
All things are given in this life which commence at our birth.
We earn and receive many charms, we surely place at heart.
In the end, value is derived from those who give a part.

Not just a coin from wallet or purse, or time that is the cost.
It is the gift of inner being that shows what is not lost.
Carried and treasured most many days in the time ahead.
Kept close, reviewed in other ways and valued for what is said.

A symbolic unwrap and taping shall show more than just suspense.
The thought and wonder awaits us all with revealing its pretense.
A cup of cheer and ornament placed enhance the whole effect.
The shine and glow of better things sweep away the old neglect.

A Holiday becomes much more when things are rough and mean.
A treasured time of greater worth. A gift from the supreme.
Little ones will always know the joys withheld inside.
If all could view the firelight and love that is implied.

A meal with courses beyond compare will end the day of gold.
For years the visions of better times show moments to unfold.
The joy and wish and care become a measure raised above.
Peace and calm will protect and shield by all there is in love.

I was determined to get through the holidays intact. That to me was a test of my endurance and fortitude. Even though things were said about me I didn't care. Let them talk. I resolved to hold my own. I wouldn't waste time defending myself from false accusations. Besides, I found out real fast who my friends were. They were the ones who did not believe a thing.

As the holidays came and went I found inner strength. Decorations and things that had always cheered me up did not equal the feelings of past years. I felt a little depressed but fought it off. At the conclusion of festivities, I went back to work. I wrote a number of poems and pieces and just felt all around better. I had very little contact with other family but decided that maybe that was for the best. I had learned over the years how to go things alone and this was just another example.

For the new year I vowed to rebuild and grow. Although that would seem an easy task, it wasn't. I knew depression was at the door. I had to learn how to chase him away. He is very persistent.

I wrote this poem one morning. I looked over to a mirror and it flowed out of me. I really like it. One of many that I wrote that I really like.

Looking Glass

Dec 15

Appearance shows what skin allows and only creates form.
Modified and altered thus from which the day we're born.
We clothe and hide the shapely mess that ego sculpts away.
Effecting change a human trait, beauty of the day.

To stand up close and look at deep yields so much more to tell.
A view for some a frightening glance upon the gates of hell.
Inner strength and failures become an outward scar or mark.
Remembered for and accepted then as character lines in dark.

A glance into your own eyes lets the view of soul come through.
It allows the person to look upon the one who brought it true.
A judgment then shall commence and trial will persist.
In the end a jury decides the sentence to commit.

No pardon or bargain can be made when final acts are done.
For in the mind the jailor walks and sentence has begun.
A time a measure of pain and sorts. A torture to behold.
Until at last the judge returns and frees the bleeding soul.

All come to court someday I fear and stand to be condemned.
A look upon the silver glass determines foe or friend.
It tells no lies and hides no truth the reality glares so deep.
For what is sown shall always be the measure that one reaps.

For this I say with sharpness tongue remember act of day.
The judge will come and look right through. He's in the mind to stay.
All will walk past your form and know not of the wretched curse.
But of your bowels a dungeon forms. The torment of this verse.

With this said and all are warned of what it all becomes.
Take heed and view the looking glass as glaring at the sun.
Shield eyes and heart and peer not true at what is shown and laid.
For it is such an image real of what your life has made.

The final words on this I know are not for me to say.
Rehearsed and kept locked up tight until your dying day.
No one can make the decision known. No other shall ever see.
You must come forth and witness it. Your soul finds destiny.

Strange Viewpoint

Everything in this section may sound odd. You must consider, though, all that has happened up to now. The events and circumstances leading up to present will always affect decisions and thoughts. No matter your intention, past and present are intertwined tightly like wound rope. Never think they are separate entities.

After going through such events, your point of view will change. You believe experience can aid the current dilemma. Lessons learned assist decision making and add a new maturity toward problems. You do not look to place blame. You seek the truth and find the reality of the answer refreshing.

Resentment

At the completion of things I would be lying to say that I have no resentment. I do. However, I realize that it has to be put into perspective with everything else. I resent years of things. I resent treatment toward me. I resent being taken for granted and the mental abuse as it were.

I resent sleepless nights and dealing with things that I should not have. I resent being handed medical and emergency situations that I didn't want to handle. I resent decisions I had to make because I had no choice. I could not debate or discuss them with anyone other than professionals at the time. I resent being blamed for things I did not do. I resent being accused of things I did not do.

A lesson is here to be learned. At the conclusion of a relationship keep one thing in mind. No one normally enters into relationships for the sole purpose of ending them. You came together for reasons of attraction or compatibility to be joined together. With that said, remember that the parting should be the same.

Leave with your head high and go forth to find your place. Heal, reflect and learn from the past, but carry forth. Resentment, anger and bitterness get everyone nowhere. Say nothing bad of the other person. Do not lie or fabricate false realities. Walk away with your heart and mind intact. When you are ready, you will find someone else.

I hold no anger or hatred. Those things are a disease which I have no time for. I only hold the thoughts of good times and remember them. No blame, no bitterness. I have learned my lessons and will continue. What I have experienced has made me a better person. That is what I know. Others may say what they please. They will eventually answer for their own words.

Time Bandit

I resent giving precious time to someone and losing that same precious time with someone else who would have appreciated it and me. The years lost are a brutal reality that I must come to terms with. It is the one thing that can never be regained once lost—time. We watch it tick by and eventually we run out of it. The day comes when we have none left. At that point we hope we made the best out of what we had. If not, it is too late.

This brings me to my next point, precious time. When you are with someone it is imperative to realize that your actions in life not only affect yourself but the one you are with. The little selfish things done will take away the gifts that were given each of you.

Don't think your actions, thoughts and motions are just concerning yourself. Remember that the cause and effect situation applies here. The decisions, judgments and attitudes will somehow place a benefit or burden on someone else. Always take into consideration the reality that simple, seemingly silly motions, reactions and efforts show forth in the course of time. Little waves upon the horizon, here and there, may become great waves and will sweep down the fiber of the relationship.

To summarize all that I said here, keep in mind a simple thank you, kiss on the cheek or rub of the back confirm that our time together is not wasted. We love and belong there. It will show you are not a time bandit.

Obstacle

Dec 16

Did you ever look straight up at a wall?
To determine why it must be mastered at all?
You know that you can not go around it or through.
You honestly know what you are intended to do.

As you climb you find you are truly alone.
You feel little objects strike your back as if stone.
It does not dismay or alter your course.
An effort involved carries on with much force.

The option to turn does not even exist.
To go back is suicidal, soon crossed off your list.
To carry on seems so brave but merely the path.
No help comes so you soon do the math.

It adds up to one thing and one thing alone.
You block out the noises carry forth like a drone.
You realize that action and progress just lay,
In the walking and stumbling carried forth on that day.

Every side has a critic and shouts things disturbed.
No point in rebutting when nothing is heard.
Judges and juries gather round, sentence quick.
Not knowing the truth but shaking a stick.

You wonder if decision was just made too fast.
Then realize that you were the one with the past.
The motion must happen and you will try so.
The scars and the marks are the force that you know.

As rocks fly quick past and arrows are shot
You look at your hands. A weapon you've not.
You draw no rifle, or pistol or bow.
Others around do the shooting you know.

You keep going on and hope that you can.
Walk through the chaos and act like a man.
Fear not an option or doubt not worth time.
It is too much to lose with a slip of the mind.

Loved ones repelled for safety and such.
Their concern is just a motion of loving with touch.
Something must happen soon as you know.
The finish is approaching for winds they do blow.

No matter the outcome, words thoughts or acts.
A simple little truth shall be known as the pact.
You did what thought best no matter the odds.
A human endeavor. Laid softly by God.

"Be grateful for what you have for another may wish to find what you take so lightly. . . ."

Reasons Why

I'm sure after reading this you are sitting there wondering why anyone would go through these things. I have asked myself that question many times. The reasons are simple. When you feel someone believes in you, you naturally reciprocate. Against all better judgment at times, you believe in them.

When you are young and naive, things do not seem wrong. They seem more natural. You have not learned any different. As you experience things in life, you find that there are many things that seem one way, but are actually another.

First Married

I realized early on that it was insanity to subject myself to these trials. I had a loyalty to her that I could not define. It was part of my codependent nature. I just never realized it at the time. The story goes like this.

When we were first married, I was immature, not that I have changed much since then. I had no idea as to the direction that I wanted to take in life. I was a confused young man. The only concrete thing in my life was Terry.

She, in her own way, was my savior. Remember, behind every great man is a great woman. She took my hand and gave me love. She was there for me when I did not have a clue. Although I struggled to define myself, she helped me. I will forever be in her debt. As the years past, I grew as a person and began to shape myself. I am a much stronger and self-confident person now.

I owe her for all of the initial support. I believed it was my turn to repay that debt as we went through things. I took her hand and lead her out of her troubled waters. I did not turn my back on her. I believed myself to be her best friend. I had faith that I would do the right thing and stand by her.

We endured many things through the years, some good, and some bad. But those who knew us have said that we had always dealt with things as a family. It is more important, though, to work through rough times. We do not have all of the answers. I can honestly say that if it were not for her, I may not be here. If it were not for me, she may not be here. We did struggle, but we will endure. Each of us in our own ways.

Kids

The next reason for sticking it out was the kids. When you have children you have an obligation to support and aid them. There are times when this is not easy, but you do it. In times of trouble you shield and protect them. They are innocent bystanders in a not-so-perfect world. I have many times put myself in harm's way on their behalf. That is what being a parent is all about.

I have seen many families break apart and become bitter. Many times I was offered an out. At no time, though, did I consider taking it. I had a greater obligation to the good of the family unit. All of us have become scarred by these events. I would be fooling myself to think otherwise. We have, however, become stronger because of these things. I know that we have been bent, and beaten. Above all, though, we have survived.

The Last Reason

It is hard to explain the last reason. It is not the fact that I liked these things. It is not that I wanted to subject myself to these things. It is more that after many years I had grown accustomed to these ways. Now I prefer quiet, uneventful times.

I have survived many years on the edge. I dealt with insanity throughout my day. The twists and turns kept me fresh. I never could handle mundane schedules. I flourish when things are impossible. Maybe this is why these things don't faze me. After numerous events and years, I've grown fond of challenges.

Codependent and Liking It

I was used to living a certain way. Relatively out of the ordinary behavior patterns were commonplace to me. I never saw the trouble as others did. I always felt that it was supposed to be that way. If I saw a problem, I would think it was not as bad as it really was. You become accustomed to things and generally accept them.

After a while you actually prefer it. Normal lifestyles are very uncomfortable. They seem distant and odd. I have a hard time to this day coping with normal and traditional environments.

I am still working on acceptance of them.

The other aspect to this is that you do not seek a better and normal existence because in your heart you do not believe that you deserve it. This self-defeating mentality creeps into your entire lifestyle. It is not so much that you do not want better. It is that you never felt that you of all people deserved better.

You don't deserve better in a million years. You believe fundamentally you go through these things because you deserve it and/or have brought these things upon yourself. In essence, they are your fault.

When you walk into a room you look around. You see all of the people. It is normal to gravitate toward those whom you would be attracted to. When instantly you eliminate the people that you do not feel worthy of being around, you limit your choices of interaction. This is what subconsciously occurs. It is an immediate and underlying reaction. I have always been that way.

I Have Always Wondered

I cannot be sure of the number of people that go through these things with mental illness in their family. I only hope that the number decreases every year. Those of us who deal with this are unique. We see sides of the human mind that not very many people are privileged to see. To know someone before all of this and then see a metamorphosis is fascinating, actually.

It is amazing to know that our minds can change and develop in various ways. Simple events in our lives can mutate and warp with little or no realization on our part. Are they chemical changes? Are they neurological? Can they be reversed?

Many questions come to my mind. Once we encounter a traumatic event, are we destined to experience these things to one degree or another? Is there a genetic link? Are some more prone to encounter these things?

I have had many questions over the years but relatively few answers. Some think that we are a developed species. I believe that we are not. We only use a minimal amount of our brains capacity. What about the rest? Will we ever fully utilize its abilities? Time will tell.

GUILT

"No pardon or bargain can ever be made when final acts are done. For in the mind the jailor walks and sentence has begun.
A time a measure of pain and sorts. A torture to behold.
Until at last the judge returns and frees the bleeding soul."

An interesting topic I must say. We all feel it everyday. Some of us just choose to ignore it. After going through all of this I have a truckload of it. Need any clean fill? Maybe it is not so clean, huh? In any case it is something that I have had to learn to come to terms with.

Why feel guilty, you ask? Good question. Why not! It is a natural emotion tied into love and caring and every other piece of baggage that we carry. However, it should be looked at through tainted eyes.

Guilt comes from wondering whether you did everything humanly possible and beyond during situations to make things right. It manifests itself in many forms. We subject ourselves to it and torture our own souls.

When in the course of events you deal with situations, crises, trauma, and many other untold things, guilt manifests itself because at any moment you are not sure if you did everything right. You tried your best. Was it good enough? When one incident occurs you think about that. When numerous ones occur, you know you did not do all things properly. You just did what you had to do. That is when the guilt builds up.

The main point here is the fact that when it all is over, you must learn to forgive yourself for being human. You know you made mistakes. You know you tried. You were not perfect. You just did what you thought best at the time. That is the sentence you have cast on yourself. Realize that your guilt is manifested from being human. Mistakes are a part of our frailties. They are not a weakness. They are essentially a fact of life.

Morning Tears

Every morning when I get up I make an unconscious decision. When I am awake enough I decide if I will cry on the way to work or not. In a split second in my mind it is decided. How do I do that, you may ask? It is simple. If my mind wanders and reflects on things that have happened and if I do not stop that from occurring, I will cry. However, if I stop it before it wanders too far, I will not.

Everyone has memories and thoughts that if left unchecked, will encircle and enslave us. The ultimate trick to healing, I have found, is to slowly bleed out the pain and horrible thoughts and memories. Slow is important.

Why slow? Well consider that if you quickly release the thoughts and emotions that have built up, you create voids and gaps in your soul and mind. More than likely you will try to fill them with false realities and ultimately have to complete the whole process all over again. When you slowly bleed clean, though, you allow the natural process of healing to occur. You will fill the voids with good things you truly desire to place there. These will cement your future. You do not repeat the process of pain. You learn to overcome it. These are just my thoughts on the matter.

IMPROVEMENT NEEDED

With everything I have been through, I started working on this topic. "How do we become better people?" The first thing is we have to let go of our past and grab onto our future. Sounds easy, right? Take it from me, the releasing of the past is the most difficult thing you will ever do. The past and all of its events and tendencies has shaped and molded us. You don't think so?

Take a simple piece of paper. Pick it up and fold it 3 times. Think about what that folded piece of paper looks like and what it means to you.

Now take another piece of paper. Give it to someone else and tell them to fold it 3 times. Let them do it anyway they want. Ask them what it looks like to them. What does it mean to them? It is the same piece of paper with the same number of folds. Yet it yields a different outcome. Why? Welcome to the world of humanity!

Experience, thoughts, the past and present issues all add up to one thing: Who we are! Improving upon that and making ourselves better is a daily chore. Inner reflection and thought added to self-realization mean taking stock in yourself. What do you think is right about you? What do you think is wrong with you? How can you fix it?

After all of this why do I think and feel this way? The truth is I never want to go back. It took me a long time to walk out of the darkness and stand upright. I'd rather not do it again. I survived to write and learn and live. I did not survive to go back.

Hidden Passages

Feb 4

Some think them a block to obstruct any view.
For others passages, with which to walk through.
A divider to some but an entrance to the rest.
Possibilities await for those who will test.

Numbered and labeled, all colors do show.
Marked by the owner. Purpose to know.
Simple or elegant, always quite real.
Decorated for Holidays, a commence and appeal.

Life places them always right in our path.
A choice to be made. A decision with wrath.
Right and wrong ventured with a turn of a knob.
Many times easy. Others a job.

We never quite know if we made the right choice.
To shout back and alter is a strain to the voice.
Did you wonder when young the purpose and stand.
Built by a person and placed there by man.

We block and we structure all things in the day.
A freedom forgiven as life slips away.
Obvious or altered most within reach.
At arm's length away, a child can teach.

Adults know nothing. Against their own view.
Little ones are wise to enter anew.
Wisdom is fleeting. Left by the side.
A map or a picture, the only real guide.

My last thoughts on this. Keep them tucked away.
Look at the writing. The truth shall display.
Open or lock as soul will surely know.
Wind will advise the path that you go.

It isn't the purpose to shield or protect.
It may be the option of love or neglect.
When right you find peace, a presence of mind.
Wrong brings a torment of pain for the blind.

DOCTORS, LAWYERS, INDIAN CHIEFS

Through all of these events I have had dealings with and experienced many different health and legal professionals. The range and scope of these individuals is an amazing display of a reservoir that this country has to offer. Often the interactions are not predetermined but random acts and acquaintances that are encountered.

In most cases you actually have no idea who you may deal with. When placed in certain situations you are just looking for help in any place that you can get it. The truth being, a social worker, a psychiatrist or psychologist may not be the best person to directly deal with the situation. They may be there, though, to lead you in the correct direction.

DOCTORS

In all of my years I have run into few types of doctors. The first type who are the ones who when they sit and talk with you, fail to listen to what you are truly saying. They have their own opinion on the situation and would rather not hear your observations. I found that very annoying.

"Hey, Doc," I would say, "I have dealt with this for six weeks now. Don't you want to hear what I have to say?"

The second type would ask for my observations or descriptions of events. I would tell the ones who were willing to listen the behavior changes, the things she said, her actions and reactions, etc. I would explain how her sleeping habits and diet and hygiene practices had changed. I would describe her verbal outbursts, her physical threats and other activities.

I would begin to tell them when I had seen all of this start to occur: What tipped me off as to the extent of severity for the year; how I anticipated the rest of the episode; what I thought she would do next. I would never say I was completely right. That is impossible. But I usually had a pretty good idea of the direction that things were going to go. That is the essence and key that I kept in my pocket that allowed me to prepare and survive.

The saying goes, "Keep your friends close and your enemies closer." I learned how true that was. Those of us who are survivors learn this. It is crucial.

Although I was never trained in the diagnosis of this kind of behavior I learned what I could do and what not to do. Certain actions and attitudes would set her off and I had to deal with accelerated anger or annoyance. You learn to step lightly, make peace when you can and duck fast when you can't.

Don't get me wrong with any of this. I have a very high degree of respect for doctors and those in the medical profession, especially those who deal with these kinds of things. It takes a great deal of patience and understanding to do this kind of work. They should be commended for the sacrifices they make for the betterment of individuals afflicted with these problems.

Lawyers

Here is an interesting topic. Lawyers are often described as parasites, ambulance chasers, and many other things. The critical thing I have found about lawyers is this: The legal system in this country is not layman user friendly. In other words, people such as myself are not accustomed to its idiosyncrasies. We struggle to understand the terms and their meaning as they apply to law. We are not stupid. Law in itself is another language and you need an interpreter. That is where lawyers come in. They explain what otherwise appears Greek to us.

In finding a lawyer, you have the problems compounded by the following: You are normally not seeking an attorney just because you are bored; you already have a legal situation that needs to be rectified. That means you are upset over the recent events to begin with. You need help and are not always sure who can best represent you in a court of law. You talk to friends and family. You discuss who they think is best and collect referrals.

With that information in your pocket you begin your quest to find the individual whom you place your trust in. I have found that if I can sit down and talk to the person that helps immensely. They should believe in your case and have ideas or thoughts on the direction that it should take in court.

A bond should form and a working relationship commence immediately. If for any reason you find the individual is not what you expect or you have doubts, you should address them abruptly. If you cannot become comfortable for any reason, then walk away before you enter into court. That is my advice.

My attorney, whom I hold in high esteem, has represented me with I believe a good amount of belief and resolve for my case. What that essentially means is that she will fight for what is felt as right. I am not saying both parties are 100% right. What I am only saying is, usually one party is more right than the other. Different circumstances and situations just complicate the entire mix of scenarios.

To put it simply, look for an attorney who you believe will represent you, listen to you, and respect your points of view. Do not just pick some one because someone else says to. Sit down and talk and learn about them. If you have to meet a few times to make up your mind, then so be it. It is better to make the right choice once than the wrong one and live with the consequences.

I wrote this poem about my attorney. It came to me one day in a courtroom. That is usually what happens.

Madam Justice

11 Aug

Forgotten books and words in stone, old thoughts and wisdom stored.
Harsh not fragile, but meant to be broken. Etched as an interpreted guide.

Proud and strong in any court, great power derived from the soul.
Her actions speak much louder than words. Her stature unsurpassed.

In a time when others crawl, upright and true she walks.
In full view and revered by most. On she climbs toward her place.

With robe of majesty she will serve, she holds all at her command.
To strike down injustice is now her way, time served well for humanity.

A swing of her gavel for sentence sake, her fathers hand on hers.
The grip of love and pride embraced. Rejoicing tears at the action.

The touch of a finger upon her shoulder, the whispering in her ear.
For daddy's girl has reached her heights, while her loving father stood so near.

Behind it all, unknown to most, a presence felt to me. His spirit has encircled her, as if wind around a tree.

The words he spoke while in her midst ring true forever more.
My little one has grown and become, a woman we all adore.

With this I leave a word of thanks. For all that she has done.
Never forget the path you chose. He always said it was the right one.

Courts and Lawyers

In all of the times I have been in court I have learned one thing. When you are in court, only speak when spoken to. Respect the judge, the other attorney and all other personnel involved. Look as presentable as possible, be polite, be courteous, be professional and above all be quiet. Do not argue, do not speak harshly, and do not interject comments. Make your points clearly and with as few of words as possible. Do not interrupt the other parties. Hopefully your lawyer will behave in the same fashion.

I only speak when asked a question or when prompted to tell about my observations or views. I await a queue from the judge and patiently remain quiet. A lot of times I will sit in the courtroom and just write. I will pick an object that I see and just write about it. That succeeds in a few things. First, I remain quiet while I am doing it. Second, I keep preoccupied and out of trouble. Third, I don't sit there and dwell on anything said about me. Last, it is a good mental exercise. It keeps my mind sharp. There are many good reasons and more why I do these kinds of things. These are just a few.

It is funny how you might think these things common sense. Take a day and sit in a court of law, though. You would be shocked at the behavior of a large percentage of the individuals. Whether male or female, it doesn't matter. I just sit and shake my head at the actions. Those who have the greatest self-control and patience will usually win or get a better dispensing in their case.

I have seen people lose cases just because they didn't sit down and be quiet. It's amazing. I saw one woman argue with a judge after she had won the case. Her lawyer told her, "Hey, be quiet, you won." She ended up with a contempt of court charge as well.

The funniest courts that I have sat in are local courts for traffic and other things. People are so creative in their stories. I was in one court room and a group of teenagers were there to face charges on destroying mailboxes in the neighborhood. This group of kids tried to outwit a judge. It was actually a beautiful thing to watch.

"Well, Judge, we didn't mean to destroy all the mailboxes. Actually, we were only after one and things kind of got out of hand." What a tremendous opening argument for defense. You can guess they didn't win. They were each issued a large fine, and they had to pay for new mailboxes for the owners.

If the comedy club in your neighborhood is booked up, take my hint, just go to local court and watch and listen. It's worth the ticket price, even if you are guilty!

Instincts and Friends

Every day we walk down paths that confuse or enlighten us. We rely on two things to help us get through it all: our instincts and friends. Instincts are imbedded in us from birth. They give us feelings and concerns about situations. They are a sort of protective trigger that keep us out of trouble if we listen to them.

However, if you choose to ignore them, you are on your own. Some of us call that the third eye. Animals have lived with them since the beginning of time. They can hear and know things long before humans have any idea.

Some people say it is intuitive. Others call it powers of observation. I prefer to consider it awareness of our surroundings and environment. Signs of trouble are always quite clear when you are able to see and are receptive to them.

> "Friends don't take each other by the hands. We carry the wounded soul to a safer place and rest it down gently. Then we guard it until it is well again. Our tears heal. That is what friends do."

Divorce

This begins a sad issue with me. Even the thought of this has brought tears to my eyes. After many years, I had begun to fight the thought of divorce. When you "love" someone so long, you hope things never come to this. I have never been a quitter. This used to be the equivalent of quitting to me. Many have told me it is not. As I healed, I began to look at this entire situation differently.

Want Better

After many years and many events, through therapy I have found that I want better. I would rather not go through these things anymore. I would rather try to make and live life as opposed to this existence. Most have said to me that they are shocked that I held on this long. I retort that when you love someone, you hold on and try to make it work. She was never a bad person. I liked her as a person. I just came to the realization that I didn't love her anymore. We were different people going different ways. It was now time to shake hands and part.

The damage done by hanging on is apparent. My therapy sessions have brought that to light. I have seen changes in myself over the last few months. I look at life and many things differently now. It is odd to wake up one morning and see the same view in a completely different way. It was as if something in me snapped.

I look at Terry from a completely different perspective. That is a very sad thing. After being together for years, we are drifting apart. I want differently then she wants. I want a fair chance for me to grow.

Do not think that I look at her with hate or dislike. I have just found that we have grown apart. I do not wish ill of her. I have supported her as best I could, but feel that I need to live life for myself rather than in the shadows of these things anymore.

There is always that fear in me of things occurring again. Without therapy or medication, I see signs. They are not full blown episodes. They are glimpses of the past. At anytime, they can happen again. We have done well over the years. I have looked out for her as best as I could. I wonder everyday if my time has passed and another is to take over where I have left off.

Therapist

It is funny to note how a therapist will not take sides. They just try to draw out of you how you feel. They ask the right questions and look over your answers. Once observed, they come back with sharper points to get to the truth.

We have discussed divorce and explored my options. The therapist asked why I held on. Why would I consider ending things now? I explained how I felt like I can do no more to aid her. I wondered if I had brought her to the end of the road that I travel. There is a fork in the road. Am I meant to go a different way then she is?

It is not that I don't care. It is more that we shall part as a couple and hopefully remain friends. That remains to be seen. I will always wish her the best. I just feel that it is time for me to find my way instead of constantly finding the way for us. She must find her own way.

I guess that is what makes this so hard. There is no animosity for her. She has always told me how she wants to hang onto me no matter what. In one way, I understand. On the other hand it is annoying. I wish she would let me go in peace. She tells me that she will make me love her again.

The problem that I have found with love is that people love each other for a lot of reasons. The thought that you can make someone love you is absurd. It is a miracle of nature, actually. People are different by nature. They come together for any number of reasons. No one really knows why. The point is that it is impossible for someone to make you love him or her. It must occur in the natural way that was intended.

A Therapist's Thanks

Aug 05

Words and thoughts expressed by some, memories and struggles to others.
A tear and emotions defined the past. Pain and release go hand in hand.

To listen and learn is her calling in life. Observance is her tool of craft.
Actions and words intertwined as one. Judgments reserved and savored.

Some look down upon the art. Others look up in wonder.
The human mind is undefined and immense, forever wild and uncontrolled. With a look and a nod, you know your place.

A word or phrase beyond acceptance.
A lift of an eyebrow or a smile on her face,
will exclaim her position quietly.

To counsel and address the issues at hand while
steer a course toward eventual health.

All seek to find the answers beneath.
Only a few even break the surface.

Time spent with her lights possibilities at hand.
Eventual happiness will be found.
I appreciate her attempts to uncover all
underlying troubles and woes.

We are quiet and crawling to get to our place,
but our tears are just as genuine
No shouting or screaming shall ever occur,
only grateful silence and peace of mind.

These simple words are my way of thanks,
as a thought for her to savor.
On trying days of strife and stress,
remember us all who you have helped

Closing Curtain

After reading all of this I am sure you are beginning to wonder how it all turned out. After years of things, court, doctors, lawyers, trials and every other nightmare you can imagine the end finally came.

Journeys are never defined by their intent. They are defined by the painful trials that we must go through to complete them. I learned from all of this that when others tell you how wrong you are, listen to your heart and soul.

The Final Custody Evaluations

If you have never been through this process let me explain it to you. It begins with one party requesting an evaluation and determination for custodial parent. Most of the time the woman ends up being the custodial parent. Why? Mainly because it is felt she will be better able to care for and raise the children. Although I agree that usually is the case, I felt I was involved with a different set of circumstances.

Once a psychologist, psychiatrist or other evaluating doctor is assigned by the court, the process runs until its completion. Either party can waive their right to fight for custody in the interim, but usually it ends with a recommendation from the doctor and then a judgment from the court.

Deciding Factor

When we were in court deciding things, the judge made it clear he wanted all bases covered. He insisted on an exam for both of us. A psychological profile that he could base his opinion on. I think his decision was fair and just. Lay all the cards on the table and see where the poker chips fall.

With everything that had happened, I was unsure of the outcome. However, I knew that I had done what I thought was best. If I was wrong then I would find out. I would have no one to blame but myself. I would stand alone with egg on my face.

Meet the Doctor

On the appointed day we all met the doctor for the first time. We all drove to meet the doctor at the same time. I went in a different vehicle, of course. I drove up, and Terry drove herself there. I played ball outside of the office with the kids for a little bit while we waited for the doctor to arrive.

I had previously agreed not to press any charges against the ex if she got out of line in the office. I said I would leave if things became intolerable. As it turned out, it was an okay meeting. I just kept my distance and went through his questions and interviews and tests.

We each took our turns respectively, either filling out

questionnaires or answering direct questions. It was a long day. When it was completed we were told that the doctor would make a visit to each home and inspect the properties.

A scheduled date was arranged and all agreed. At this point I wasn't sure of what to expect. I figured that I had come this far, so why not continue walking this path? I marked the date down and awaited the next step.

Every day I looked over the situation. I couldn't figure out if something was wrong with how or what I thought. I only knew that I had feelings and insights that others either chose to ignore, or weren't able to see. At least that is what I thought. Right or wrong would be determined soon.

As the time passed, I sent paperwork and notes and other things to the doctor. He said send anything that I thought illustrated my case. So I did. Everything and anything I could find. That added to my stance. I read things again and realized how I did what was right for me. Was it right for my kids? That is always something that bothers parents, isn't it? Do we always do things that are best for our children?

The day came when the tours of the houses was scheduled. I received a call from the doctor that he was on his way. I left work and headed home. I had hoped not to find a disaster area when I arrived

I was glad to find only a minimal amount of clutter around and proceeded to clean the few things that I saw. The doctor came and we began to talk. He inspected the entire house. He walked through each of the bedrooms as well as the kitchen. He then decided to speak to each of us individually. I went into the bedroom with the youngest and awaited my turn.

The kids went first and when he finished he spoke to me briefly. It was a much shorter visit than I would have anticipated. When it was completed they all went over to the ex's house. I stayed and awaited some word or outcome. I thought maybe the oldest would have some news for me when he returned.

After two hours he came home and informed me that there were outbursts and words between the doctor and the ex. I thought, how can she put a nail in her own coffin? In any case, this round was over and further interviews and discussions were to follow.

Waiting Game

It seemed like eternity for any communication from the doctor. He seemed to slowly taste and savor each word he reported. I waited and wondered what he thought. Had I made a good impression? Did I state my case? What if anything did I do wrong? Many things went through my head.

If nothing else I thought about what would happen either way. If I was deemed the custodial parent, what would I do? How would I handle transitions? What should I prioritize? What would be my ultimate course of actions?

If I wasn't deemed custodial parent what would happen? How would we talk everyday? Would she let me talk over the phone? Would she interject and control every word spoken on the phone? I dreaded the thought but knew it was a possible reality. I had to prepare for that possible outcome, as scary as it was. What else could I do? I sat and waited and hoped and prayed.

Imagine

The best way for me to describe how I felt is imagine someone hiking up the tallest mountain in the world. Struggling and climbing over every rock. Their knees scraped and bleeding and sore. Tired and cold and hungry yet still going on. Determined to get to the top because they feel what they search for is there. They won't know until they get there.

Here I was. I climbed up from the cavern that used

to be my life. I survived many years of a bipolar existence with my ex. I knew I had to do this. I climbed mountain after mountain. I was tired both mentally and physically. I had to climb, though.

If after I arrived at the top I found emptiness, then that was going to be my reward. That was what I deserved. If I found a better place, then my journey was worth every bit of this. Until now, I really didn't have answers. I had a lot of questions and no real direction. I just knew the past was the past. The future is ours for the taking, though.

The Report Has Arrived

One afternoon I received a phone call from my attorney. I was informed the report was in. I was asked if I would like to read it. Most assuredly, I said. Every torrid little detail struck all of the curious nerves in my body.

I received a copy of the report and began to read through it. Details and specifics were interesting and disturbing at the same time. I learned what a professional thought of the situation. In looking back, it really tied some loose ends I had always had. Sometimes you really don't understand things. You just think you do.

With every page I learned about myself and my ex. I learned how we each did on the individual testing. I also learned what each of our behavioral tendencies actually meant. Why we act the way we do. I read all of the interviews with any family and friends that were given as references.

I read all of the things said about me. I thought some were questionable but it is water under the bridge. When someone has never met me, how can they say something like that? I would rationalize all of this.

I found it interesting to see what was listed for both of our interviews. I read them and wondered what else I was thinking and forgot to say. Would it help? Would it hurt? Why were some people not included in her section of interviews? Why not more family? I knew why. I wondered if the doctor knew why. I would imagine he could figure it out.

I read all of my test scores and glanced over why the doctor thought I scored that way. I learned a lot from the report. I read about what he thought about my observations. How accurate or inaccurate he thought any were.

It was a worthwhile report. Not because of any individual thing it said. I simply think it gave a pretty good overview of the entire situation. I think, in a nutshell, the doctor said with medical, psychological, and realistic terms what I had been saying all along in my simplistic way.

The court appointed him. The court assigned him. The court defined his role. Now the court had to accept or deny his findings. I had done my part up to now. I came to court to seek justice. Would it be found or would another chapter in all of this be written because of denial?

If nothing else came of this, I felt better. I had stood and said the truth. I had endured and laid at the feet the reality of the situation. Now what? Law is law. I am only a pawn in this, trying to survive like anyone else. I fought for what I thought was right.

In a Nut Shell

The best areas I found were the sections on what the doctor thought about the ex. How did he see her? How would he describe her behavior? How wrong was I? Did I need more help than I thought I did? Was I the one with the warped sense of reality?

After reading paragraphs assessing her condition I found a few things out. His opinions lent credence to all of the beliefs I had up to this point. He diagnosed her with a severe Bi-Polar disorder. That made me feel better, that maybe I was right. Others who constantly blamed me for things were wrong. I just breathed a sigh of relief.

Many things were explained in his words. Mis-diagnoses and past mistakes lent us to struggle through things. Many years ago she was diagnosed correctly. Then she was mistreated and mishandled. Again and again it had occurred. It was such a shame. Somehow, though, we managed to make it work and survive.

Now what, though? I had the divorce settled. I had the grounds that I had asked for, extreme cruelty. I had a report in my hands that said I should be the custodial parent. I lived on my own with the kids and liked it. I should be as happy as can be, right?

Something to all of this was missing, though. I felt that even though my actions had been vindicated, there was something more I was seeking. I was climbing the mountain against all odds. However, I wasn't in awe of the view I found when at the top.

After all, I was going to have the kids to raise. Yet I was still waiting for the hammer to drop. Once all of these facts hit home and she realized her new position, she would switch behavior from denial to anger. That is what I waited for. I had that feeling in the pit of my stomach.

I couldn't do anything about it. I proceed and tried to make the best off it. Sounds familiar, doesn't it? In any case a return to court was in order. Now I had the material I had waited for. I would request custodial parent rights. I didn't ask for anything more than what I thought was right.

Every so often I would sit and reread the reports. The profiles and testing descriptions and their outcomes had brought hope and faith back into my life. The light at the end of the tunnel had just become much brighter. I would look at the youngest and be thankful that someone had listened.

Up to this point I was still being judged. Things were

thought and said. Yet those who were saying them never really looked at the facts. They only viewed scattered situations and words. The whole picture was only being viewed by those impartial and willing to actually look. Family will never look at matters impartially. They only view things through rose-colored glasses. I guess that is how feuds start, huh?

Next Phase

A new plan was now in order. I had to sit down with my attorney and petition the court for custodial parent. What would that mean? Well, to be precise I would have to file a motion to obtain a court order to transfer the children from one school to another.

That would entail another visit to court, another appearance before the judge and possibly a trial. I had been down this same road before. I knew what to expect. It was obvious to me she would fight this tooth and nail. I suspected as much. That would lead to another series of situations, words and problems. At least now, though, they were coming in intervals and not every day.

How can you blame anyone for fighting for their kids or what they themselves believe in? You can't. You can only fight for what you believe in. Somehow, someway, in court it will get decided. Outside arguments are not worth the time.

It is funny how you grow through time and learn that experience and pain yield tolerance. The more that happened, the less of an effect it would have. Occasional annoyances were to be dealt with. When things became intolerable you just learn to walk away and return when you are in a better frame of mind. That way all is handled more rationally and not in an emotional state.

Final Battle

Open and shut case, right? Not quite. I walked into the court waiting room to find her family there waiting for me. I would be polite but firm. The accusations were thrown at me. I threw them back.

"We know she is high strung . . ." That is an understatement that I will never forget. With all I put up with and endured I walked away from them. I sat as far from them as I could.

I was outnumbered but not outgunned. I stood alone through all of this and refused to back down.

Our lawyers began the negotiations and my attorney would sit by me occasionally. Our brief discussions went well and we handled things calmly. The other side, however, was constantly in turmoil.

Now I intended to stand firm. I would be fair and allow as much visitation as possible, but I wanted custodial parenting rights. I was not leaving without them. I had the information to back my belief.

Lawyers and judges argued and discussed. They negotiated and bantered back and forth. I had come this far. I saw the gold ring. I knew what was right for my children. I didn't endure all of this to back down now.

After a bit my lawyer came back with a proposal. It gave me custodial rights and an offering for a visitation schedule. I intended on cleaning up the visitation process anyway. I heard screams and insults and accusations.

I went to get a cup of coffee. My lawyer asked me what I thought. I said no matter what happens, thanks for your efforts and what shall happen is out of my hands. I did what I thought was right.

I had my coffee in my hand and waited patiently. A family member of hers came over and began to ask me questions. I answered them respectfully but honestly. I drank my coffee. I ate 2 bananas that I had bought and waited.

My lawyer came back and stood in front of me.

"You won. Let's get out of here!"

Good answer, I thought. As I took the elevator down to a lower floor I heard screaming and carrying on. My lawyer looked at me. I just replied yes, that is her and her attorney.

I left and went straight home. This would begin a new saga for myself and my kids.

I had walked the walk.

Final Comments

I look back over the years and cannot believe all that has transpired. It has changed my life forever. I look at everything entirely different now. The times that transformed me are starting to fade into passing thoughts. I value some things differently than others and I tend to lead a more simplistic lifestyle.

Money and possessions are meaningless in the scheme of things to me. What matters most is my immediate family. I look at everything from that vantage point and make my decisions accordingly.

I place no value in what others think of me anymore. They only judge me by their perceived notions of my actions. They have no real knowledge of my trials. My victories and defeats are my own.

I cannot claim much from all of these events. I can only say that through it all, I survived and persevered. I survived the test and did what had to be done. I realize what has happened to me. There were many things that cut me deep through the years, but now I only see the scars. I find it funny how I never felt the knife.

This is a portion of a note that I sent someone. I think it sums up how I feel about things.

"To go through these things and not cry would be impossible. Do not think that it makes me less of a man, though. In fact I think it makes me more of one because I love the woman in my life that much harder and that much truer. I care so I cry. It tears out my soul sometimes. But I stand and go back for more. That is what makes me a man. To know what it will do to me, but to go back and do it for those that I love."

The problem with all of this is that is you never take into consideration what it does to yourself. That has been my problem. I always disregarded my own welfare for the good of the family. It never dawned on me the damage I was doing. Wisdom comes at a very high price. Doesn't it?

Life's Room

Dec 29

Eventually we are gathered up for all to view. Our life yields a room with the value as the sum. All corners piled high with debris and remnants. The rusty shelves filled with the paths that we chose. Old cabinets are stocked with lost thoughts and ideas. Crevices and shadows hiding long-forgotten pain and sorrow.

As you enter the room, the lack of light surrounds you. The darkness becomes a blanket to be wrapped tightly over the shoulders. The one lamp in the corner yields such a minimal amount of glow. You strain to see all contents.

A glimmer of hope reflects in the cabinet against the wall. A shattered dream is on the floor. The pile of broken hearts under the dust is neatly stacked. Pictures show the memories and thoughts. A movie runs endlessly on the wall displaying the best of times. A pitcher full of hopes sits on the lone table surrounded by numerous glasses, some half filled, some half empty.

A small wash tub collects your lifelong tears of joy and sorrow. The failures are stored in a wooden case. They are locked to be kept out of sight. The triumphs are mounted and framed on all walls, displayed proudly to show accomplishments.

The rug on the floor is woven from the strands and fiber of character. A pattern was created by the journeys and adventures. A little candle burns by the door. The flame dances to show the flow of life and love.

A photo album of thoughts and memories is open and leaning against the wall in the corner. Its pages are shifting constantly as the owner remembers things from the past.

The lack of furniture leads you to know that you are only welcome to visit. You absorb it all in and feel the life of the occupant. Everything from the warmth of happiness to the cold chill of neglect meld gathered together. All these emotions and more surround you.

You stand there watching the commotions and activities. A constant symphony of past and present life. Although you are intrigued by the items surrounding you, it is time to leave. In an instant you have absorbed all that was involved in the life. The acts and actions will not leave your head as you walk away, confused yet enlightened at the reflections of your own mortality. Spirit breathes again in the heart you considered dead.

No name has been applied to everything experienced. It is not needed. You attach your own. You realize you have just entered the corners of your own mind and soul. That is why they were all so familiar. You could not stay. A visit with our past is a good thing. To reside there is dangerous.

You realize the visions and dreams you have discarded are all collected here. You take heed. The lessons learned show you a great collection of epiphanies. Your life as it is, is not what you intended. What you can and must do to correct it is at your own hands. You proceed to the future with that thought in mind. You begin to rewrite the contents of the room to fit your new dreams. You are now on track. Your soul warms and glows again.

TATE PUBLISHING & *Enterprises*

Tate Publishing is commited to excellence in the publishing industry. Our staff of hightly trained professionals, including editors, graphic designers, and marketing personnel, work together to produce the very finest books available. The company reflects the philosophy established by the founders, based on Psalms 68:11,

"THE LORD GAVE THE WORD AND GREAT WAS THE COMPANY OF THOSE WHO PUBLISHED IT."

If you would like further information, please call
1.888.361.9473
or visit our website
www.tatepublishing.com

TATE PUBLISHING & *Enterprises*, LLC
127 E. Trade Center Terrace
Mustang, Oklahoma 73064 USA